Selling Local Advertising

Includes Bonus Section:
   Seminar Selling;
The Best Kept Secret To Creating Immediate Profits In Your Advertising Business

By Claude Whitacre

Copyright ©2013 Claude Whitacre
All rights reserved.
ISBN-13: 978-1481862592
ISBN-10: 1481862596

Dedication

This book is dedicated to three mentors I have had that shaped my business and my life.

Julius Toth taught me more about selling than anyone. His sales prowess is mythic. In one year, he was the top distributor for a company with over 100,000 distributors. He isn't a person; he's a force of nature. He has proven himself to be a good friend, and I'm glad he counts me as one of his.

Bob Durbin is simply the best man I know. He taught me how to do business with the customer in mind. He showed me what you become when you dedicate yourself to being a good person. He is genuine to a fault. And I would be a different person if I never met him.

My Dad was a blue collar electrician for the Ford Motor Company in Berea Ohio. He had his share of defects; but I'll say this; he never lied to me that I know of. He never cheated anyone, and always treated his family well. He was always willing to help me in any way I asked, and he was damn good at what he did. I don't think Dad really understood what I did for a living, but it didn't matter. Cancer killed him slowly and viciously. Every time you hear about someone dying from cancer, they are called "brave and courageous". It's not bravery to suffer. But my dad didn't complain until the very end. He was a Marine when he was young. He was always a Marine. I miss him terribly.

My wife Cheryl... What can I say? I chose well. If you ever watch me get a stupid grin on my face for no reason, I'm thinking of her. The joke is, either I did something wonderful in a previous life, or she did something terrible... because we are together. Anyway, it's a pleasure growing old with her. And knowing she feels the same way is better than any other gift.

CONTENTS

Acknowledgements ----------------------------- i

Why Sell Advertising? ------------------------ 7

Selling Advertising VS The
Business Of Advertising. ---------------------- 9

Image Ads VS Response Ads. ----------------- 13

The Real Reason Ad Reps Fail. --------------- 17

Rustlers VS Ranchers ------------------------- 21

Smack The Prospect In The
Side Of The Head! ---------------------------- 25

Prospecting; --------------------------------- 29

Referrals ------------------------------------ 51

The Value Of One Additional Client --------- 65

Additional Ways To Get
That First Ad Sale. ---------------------------- 67

The Best Way To Build Your Business ------ 71

How To Absolutely Beat
Your Competition ----------------------------- 75

"Selling Is A Numbers Game"? ---------------- 79

How To Think Like A Marketer --------------- 85

Great Advertising Will Not
Overcome Bad Marketing – *Ever*---------------89

How To Get Your Client To
Think Like A Marketer-------------------------93

Qualifying Questions;---------------------------95

Are You Selling A Contract
For 13 Weeks, 12 Months, Or
Any Other Bulk Sale (and you
should)...Read This!-------------------------------99

Advertising Media; Strengths
& Weaknesses-----------------------------------103

The "Advertising Budget"-----------------------111

Always Think "Return On
Investment...ROI"---------------------------------115

Tracking Ad Results. And How
To Get Your Clients To Do The Same.--------117

What Is Total Customer Value (TCV)?-------121

Answering Objections----------------------------131

The Master Level Closing Technique---------155

Visit with ideas----------------------------------169

In A Sales Slump? Here's The Way Out-------175

The Reality Of Goal Setting...
And How To Really Reach Your Goals---------179

Collecting The Money-----------------------------183

Selling Advertising With Seminars----------------185

Recommended Reading;----------------------------209

ACKNOWLEDGMENTS

I wrote the book myself. Hunter Miller assembled the chapters and helped with proofreading.

Amazon.com has a program called CreateSpace that makes publishing incredibly easy, and that's the method we used for this book.

My wife Cheryl helps in ways I can't even describe. She patiently listens to each new speech, technique, or training method. She gives me her opinion and her support.

I've made more than my share of mistakes in life. But in finding a great wife? I chose well.

And the fact that she feels the same way makes life so much more fun.

For Advertising Sales Managers Only.

Wouldn't it be great if you could give your new rep a *Fast Start* to give them a huge advantage over their competition?

What you have in your hands right now will make your job easier.... because it makes your rep's job easier. This book will shorten the learning curve.

With your help, we can change the client's image of your advertising rep from "Another Ad Rep" to "Welcomed Trusted Advisor". Some of the difference is approach... and most is the *depth of knowledge* possessed by the rep. My experience with advertising reps is that they tend to be bright and creative people. That's why they were attracted to advertising sales in the first place. It's just a matter of learning what works.... what works both in *selling* advertising.... and what works in *advertising itself.*

The first two weeks of a new rep's career are the most important. Work habits will be formed, attitudes will be created, and the new guy/girl is subjected to all the bad habits of the older reps. My suggestion is to have new rep keep records of every call, canvassed call, presentation, and total sales volume.

And you inspect their figures.
What gets inspected...... gets done.
What gets measured....... can be improved.

Personally, I would give each new hire a copy of this book. They will see it as a benefit of working with you, and you'll soon see results from your new person using the ideas on these pages.

If you hold regular sales meetings, any chapter of this book would serve as the basis of a lively sales meeting. You have more than a year's worth of weekly meeting material in this book. I would have the rep use a transparent highlighter to mark the most relevant parts of the book. Several readings are needed. This isn't a book you read, it's a book you study.

A very popular method of prospecting is handing out copies of my book **The Unfair Advantage Small Business Advertising Manual** to clients and prospects. They are inexpensive (We give generous quantity discounts), and explain most of the concepts needed to run profitable ads.
Your clients will appreciate the gesture, they will learn more about effective advertising, and will be *pre-sold on buying advertising from your reps*. Just go to www.claudewhitacre.com to learn more.

You are in a unique position. There is much you can do for your reps that can't be delivered from a book... *any* book.

I don't have your experience. You have knowledge specific to your media, market, economy, and media-specific objections and concerns. You'll know about your rep's personalities, motivations, quirks, beliefs, and histories.

One person can change the life of your new rep. One person has the ability to show the new rep that cold calling is not a death sentence...... clients are actually human beings..... and that their Sales Manager is looking out for their best interests.

One person can be credited for leading the new person to professional success in their new career. One person can show the new rep the tools and techniques they need to succeed. That person is you....... and you have one of the tools *in the palm of your hand*.

A warning about this book;
I write the way I talk. You'll soon see that I talk in declarative sentences. It's just a faster way of giving advice than being more "Warm & Fuzzy". My main purpose here is to make you more money. Really. Sometimes that means a little tough love.
I've used "he" more than "she" in the text. Frankly, I'm too lazy to count all the times I've used the words, and divided by two. To be fair, I use the word "he" whether it's describing a good or bad person. If I'm talking about a real person, I always use the correct gender. In my next book, I'll use "she" more than "he"... fair enough?

I am currently selling advertising as a profession, and I have thoroughly field tested every idea you find here. Anymore, I don't read books by experts who have never done what they are teaching. Most of these books are a waste of time, I find. But here is why you will want to read this book;
I am an expert salesperson. For over 20 years, I've sold in people's homes. I was great at it and made a ton of money. Then I opened a retail store, tested advertising ideas there, and kept records of my results. In the last 8 years in retail, we averaged an 81% increase in sales each year. So I know how to sell... as you'll see. I also know how to advertise profitably. I know how advertisers think.. and how

they buy advertising. Since selling is really just seeing things from the client's point-of-view... and matching your offer to that client... this information will be indispensable to you.

Currently, I own an advertising company called Local Profit Geyser, selling to small business owners. I also own a successful retail store where I test all of my advertising ideas.

Here's another reason you'll learn more from me than from an "Advertising Sales Trainer"; You are not locked into techniques *just* from the "selling advertising" profession. You are not restricted to copying sales methods only learned in the advertising industry. Almost every method I've learned about advertising, selling, and marketing... I've learned from industries completely different than my own. These ideas are then translated into profitable ideas in my business, and then taught to others. That's why some of these ideas will be unfamiliar to you... they aren't originally from your industry.

So why am I writing this book? My store and advertising business are still making us a good living, and I'll keep them as long as my speaking schedule permits. Frankly, I just like talking to fellow business owners and professional

salespeople more than I enjoy talking to retail consumers. There, I said it.
I've bought hundreds of thousands of dollars in advertising. I've tested the results. I know what works and what doesn't. I can clearly see advertising from both a client's and ad rep's point-of-view. That's far more profitable (to you) than from just a seller's point-of-view. I know how your prospects and clients think. I know how they *buy*...... I *am* one, after all.

I've given hundreds of seminars on local advertising, and I wrote **The Unfair Advantage Small Business Advertising Manual**. I've talked to thousands of advertisers. They tell me what they like in a rep, and what just makes their *blood boil*. They tell me the objections they give, and I've tested what works to answer their concerns. I've also interviewed dozens of top advertising reps. From all of this emerges a picture of what will work for you. Then I've tested these techniques. Everything you will read is proven profitable. No theory. For the price of a sandwich, (OK, a BIG sandwich!), you are getting the real deal. We won't be talking about what we *think should* work.... or repeat what *sounds* good, We'll be solely concentrating on what *works*.

But, enough from Claude. Let's talk about *you*.

Why Sell Advertising?

If you just started in your career, I have good news for you. You're in a unique position. Advertising is one of the very few products that creates more (for the client) money than it costs. And you are one of two people that can influence the value of what you sell (you and your client).

Here's what attracted me to sales; You don't sweat. There is little risk of physical injury. And I get paid the same way CEOs get paid... based on what I produce. And here is something I promise you; If you are generating profit for your company, your job is *secure*. If you are generating a profit for your client... your business is *secure*.

Here's why advertising is such a great field; You are talking to business owners who are used to making decisions. This isn't "one shot selling". Relationships are formed. Selling becomes more "giving advice" than making a sale. You will learn more about human nature while selling than in any other profession. You will learn more about how business works and selling advertising, than selling any other product or service. Both of these areas will help you in your life in profound ways.... all good.

Selling Advertising VS The *Business* Of Advertising.

I have a vast library of books on advertising, selling, and marketing. Almost every book on "how to sell advertising" so far is missing one key point; It's far easier to sell advertising when you have a clientele of satisfied advertisers that are bragging about how well their ads are working. If you sell an ad... and it generates $3 for every $1 in ad cost... how hard will it be to sell that *second ad*? Not hard at all. And this book will show you ways to sell that *first* ad.

You will not need to learn the business of every client you have. Fortunately, advertising principles are pretty universal. At the back of this book, I have listed recommended reading. For under $100 at www.amazon.com you can have a small but concentrated library on advertising.

Business owners tend to advertise in several media, or they don't advertise at all. So you are likely to have several other reps competing for the client's business. This is to your advantage.
Since most ads are easy to find, you simply go to the business owner that is advertising with someone else, and they are very likely to buy your offer too. Business owners that are currently using *any* advertising are infinitely more likely to buy your media too... at least a trial run.
They don't need to be sold on the idea of advertising. Eighty percent of the work is already done for you..... by the other rep. Of course, we'll also cover selling ads to the prospect that *never* advertises.

If you take the time to work with the advertiser... building ads that produce results... helping them improve ads that fail.... and sharing with them what works with other ads you've produced.... I promise you this; You will be the only one. No other rep is taking this route. All of them are selling advertising as if it were a commodity. Eventually the advertiser may cut ads out of their budget. Who are they going to keep? You. No businessperson drops an ad that generates $2 for every $1 invested in the ad.

The odds are very strong that your prospect has never read a single book on advertising, and is basing his advertising decisions on what other reps have told him, what his brother-in-law told him, and what he has seen in the movies. Most ad reps also never read a single book on advertising. Would you trust the advice of a doctor that never read a single *medical* book?

Between you and the client, don't you think that at least *one* of you should have an idea of how to make his ads pay?

When you meet a prospect, you have zero control over what he knows or believes (big difference between *knowing* and *believing*) about advertising. You have 100% control over what you know about advertising and how you can help the client make his ads pay.

"Winning isn't everything. Wanting to win is"

-Catfish Hunter

Image Ads VS Response Ads.

Ad reps love image ads. Image ads are the ones you see in national magazines that build Brand Awareness. Their purpose is to make the consumer feel better when they think of the brand name. Examples are ; "Have it your way" by Burger King, Prudential Insurance's "Own a piece of the rock", Chevrolet's "Like a rock", and Motel 6's "We'll leave the light on for ya".
Thanks to **Selling Air** by Bob Diamond for the examples)

Brand awareness ads *work*.

These ads pre-condition the consumer to more easily accept local ads that actually sell the products.

Image ads sell the company *name*. Response ads sell the *product*. Which would you rather sell if you were the client?

Ad reps love this type of ad for a reason: The sales can't be tracked... because the ads create no sales. So the advertiser continues to buy the ads... without expecting an immediate result. Also ad reps (and ad agencies) get to concentrate on being creative rather than producing sales results. Frankly, this type of ad is just more fun for the ad agency.

National companies, with dealer networks, *like* this. The dealers in their network then advertise with response ads locally, and the image ads help the response ads work better.

The problem is that occasionally, you'll meet a business owner that thinks that brand awareness ads are what local advertising *is*. So they run these ads, get no sales, and then blame... *you*.

Response ads are where the prospect responds to the ads by coming into the store, calling on the phone, or going online (depending on what the ad directs them to do). Generally, the purpose of the ad is to cause the reader/listener to come in the client's store/business and *buy*.

These ads create sales. The results can be measured. Here's another difference; Image ads don't generate sales, but response ads will generate a positive brand image almost as well as the image ads themselves.... and at the same time, pay for themselves and produce a profit for the client.

All infomercials are response ads. All QVC or Home Shopping Network ads are response ads.

Almost all of your clients will be local. Almost all of your clients will be dealers looking for sales.

Response ads that also create the desired image... are where the money is... for the client.

Getting advice?
You will be getting advice on advertising, and how to sell advertising, from several sources. Much of the advice will contradict what you read here (especially from business owners that never advertise). Consider this; How successful are they? If they give you an idea, have they used it themselves?... and what was the result?

If they tell you an idea won't work, how do they *know*?

Some of the most dangerous advice comes from well meaning people who think that selling and advertising *should* work a certain way. A customer *should* buy this, and the customer is an idiot for saying "No".

Trying to make clients *think the way you do* is hard work, an uphill climb, and unrewarding.

Working *with* the advertiser... *matching the way they think*... both of you working to make the ads profitable, and offering ways to increase their business... is fun, stress free, and almost effortless. Choose your path.

The Real Reason Ad Reps Fail.

The first time I spoke to a group of ad reps, I learned a very valuable lesson.
I joined a group of reps for breakfast at a hotel. It was the wrong table. It was the *bitching* table.

For about half an hour, I got to hear how the *company* was doing everything wrong. Everything was either the company's fault... or the customer's fault. Oh Joy.

One guy said "Customers don't *get* this business. I was talking to an advertiser the other day, and he told me that the ad wasn't making him any money. I told him that *my* job is to get the customer to his door. What happens after that is *his* business". Then he looked at me and said "Right?"

I said "No. You *can* sell that way... but what if you designed an ad that *actually made people want to buy his product?* He would stay a client-for-life. You just need to see it from his point of view."

He looked at me like was from Mars, and said "I don't know what the hell you are talking about"... and he walked away. After the seminar, we shook hands... he wasn't a bad guy.

Unfortunately, this guy was stuck in the "We sell ad space" rut. If you think that way, your career will be filled with cold calling, convincing people against their will, competition stealing your clients, and being perceived as a pest.. Selling will be *exhausting.*

This is why reps fail; Not seeing the advertising from the client's point of view... not concentrating on helping the client sell more of his product or service. This "Us VS Them" attitude is still pervasive in all types of sales. It is perpetuated by people that don't know how to sell.

Your client's success is *your* success.

It's still common for ad reps to do one-shot-selling. They show up at a business. Give a short presentation, and leave. The business owner either bought... or they didn't. This actually has merit if you have an unlimited number of prospects, or if you are selling a special project and won't be in the area long. But it isn't much fun.

What is your responsibility?
To make the prospect *want* to do business with you.... and *want to continue* to do business with you. That's what this book is about.

"It's not who you are. It's what you do that defines you"

-Batman

Rustlers VS Ranchers

I was selling vacuum cleaners in people's homes for several years. I studied selling as an art. I talked to people who were making huge incomes from their selling. And I met Julius Toth.

At the time (maybe the early 1980s), Julius owned a small retail store selling vacuum cleaners in a lower middle class area of Barberton, Ohio. He was selling about a million dollars in vacuum cleaners a year. His selling prowess was *mythic*. We found that we read the same books, used many of the same methods, and had a similar philosophy on life. We became friends almost instantly.

We would meet every Monday for breakfast to share ideas, and motivate each other.

One day at breakfast, I asked Julius what the difference was between what he did & what I did. He gave it some thought and said "Let's imagine this was the Old West. You are a cattle rustler. Every day, you go out looking for stray cattle. You find them, put your brand on them, and sell them. Every day, you do the same thing. Every day you wake up thinking about your next head of cattle. Me?... I'm a rancher. I have a ranch. I have cattle. I have a *herd*. I feed them, water them, and keep them warm at night. I nurture them, fatten them, and breed them. Every day my herd grows. Every day you start with *nothing*. Every day I start with a *herd*."

I *got* it. His way was better.

It's all about the herd. Find people you want to work with and then *court* them. There will be prospects that buy right away... and people you won't want to work with. The rest will be people that will slowly come around. People buy at different speeds. They make decisions at different speeds. It's worth it to keep after them. I would be surprised if you don't get 80% of them eventually. How to find prospects and grow them into clients is what we'll discuss now.

Let's imagine that you are not married, and are looking. Can you imagine just walking up to someone and saying "Hi. You're cute. Will you marry me?"

The answers would always be "No", you would soon become depressed... and you would eventually stop asking.

But people get married *every day*. How is this possible?
They *court*. They make small gestures to each other that shows interest and deepens a bond. Eventually that bond become nearly unbreakable.

The same process happens in business relationships. If you find a business owner that you want as a client, just keep at it. Offer suggestions, give information, send articles that apply to them, and don't give up.

Amazingly, people will warm up to you... you'll become a welcome guest (instead of a pest)... and they will start *listening*.

"Perhaps I am stronger than I think"

-Thomas Merton

Smack The Prospect In The Side Of The Head!

OK, not really!
Picture this: You walk into a store, and the clerk asks "May I help you?". What do you say? "No, I'm just looking". In fact, it's hard to say anything else. We are conditioned to respond in certain ways to certain stimulus. (I promise this will be beneficial. Stick with me!)

If I ask you "How are you?" you'll say "Fine" or "Fine, and how are you?". These are social lubricants. They make communication more frictionless, and require no thought.

My doctor asked me (when he walked in his exam room) "Hi, how are you?". I asked "Out of 100 times you ask that, how many say 'Fine'?". He thought for a second and said "80-85 percent". I said "How many are actually *fine* when you see them?". He laughed and said "I never thought of it. Almost none."

Why do you need to know this?

Because when you are prospecting..... it's easy to fall into asking questions in a way that practically forces the prospect/client to say "No"
For example, if you call and start the conversation with "I'm Bob with XYZ corporation, I'm doing a marketing survey, may I ask... hello? Hello?" (That's me hanging up)

Business owners are conditioned... until it has become a strong habit, to hang up on telemarketers.

Sometimes they are rude, sometimes not. But they aren't listening after the first five or ten seconds. They fall back on auto-pilot. We all do it.

When a customer walks in my store, I walk out from the back room and say "I'm here to serve! What can I do for you?" and I wave my arm as I say "I'm her to serve". I don't yell, but you can't ignore me. It's impossible to say "I'm just looking" after you meet me.

So my suggestion is to avoid saying the same thing they hear from every other person bothering them on the phone. Now let's talk about prospecting.

"Positioning: When an angry dog runs at you, clap your hands, smile, and say 'Here Boy!'"

-Claude Whitacre

Prospecting;

Let's quickly define what we mean by prospecting. Most trainers discuss ways to get in front of a prospect... *any* prospect. This has merit. If you keep busy enough, some of the people you see will buy. A few will even buy right away. It's called *cold calling*. It usually starts with you walking into a store or business and asking "Is the owner here? Could I speak to them?" and then you introduce yourself.. show your program... and *Pray*.

Companies love cold calling. They teach it. Why? Because…

1) They don't have to do it themselves.

2) It's incredibly simple & easy to teach

3) They don't know a better way, it's what they were taught.

4) They don't have to do it themselves. (I *know* I said it twice)

Cold calling really works. If you have nearly unlimited prospects (tens of thousands in your area), you simply call on the phone, and give a benefit statement like "We can put your ad in front of customers for 3 cents apiece. Would you like to hear more?". I'm not kidding. If you call 100 businesses a day, you'll get a "Yes" from one or two. Plenty to keep you busy. And make no mistake, these customers are ready to buy... they were ready before you called. You just *found* them.

One of the most powerful phone presentations I ever had was this: "We sell long distance for 4 cents a minute. Do you want to hear more?". That's all he said. I said "Yes", because he hit a need I had, and the timing was right. Unfortunately, I found out that the claim wasn't true, so the call ended abruptly.

But he *had* me. The speed of calling is the key.

The whole process is outlined brilliantly in the book *High Probability Selling* by Jacques Werth and Nicholas Ruben. The reason it works is that you don't care what the answer is when you ask the first question on the phone. You are *sorting*.... not selling.

You might call and ask "I can deliver your best sales message to your market for three cents each. Do you want to hear more?". If you work in a big city, this will get you to motivated, smart, and turned-on buyers of advertising. But you'll run through a lot of names until you get a client.

Think about this; Today... there are between ten and one hundred people, in your area, who really want to buy what you have. The timing is *perfect*. You can make a darn good living just *finding* them. Cold calling... by phone... with a quick message... is the way to do it. You'll dig through a lot of dirt... but you'll find the diamonds.

By the way, if you are going to cold call every small business in your area, just go to www.infousa.com You can buy compiled lists of prospects cheap... in a format that makes them easy to call.

There are several avenues you can take to prospect

cold. You can send E-Mails, phone, FAX (not recommended unless they're already a client), direct mail, or in person.

Here is something to think about when planning your prospecting:

What is the easiest thing in the world to get rid of?
An E-Mail.

Second easiest thing to get rid of?
A letter.

Third easiest thing to get rid of?
A phone call.

Now, what is the *hardest* thing in the world to get rid of?
A *Body*.

There is magic in Just Showing Up.
You may be seeing them at the "Magic Moment" when they are thinking about advertising.
From the moment I married my wife, we thought about buying life insurance. We talked about it. I said "Honey, our wedding was in the paper, somebody will call. We'll buy from the first one who calls". Nobody called.

I opened my store. I said "Honey, the store opening is in the paper. Surely an insurance salesman will call now". Nope. Nobody called. Even the guy I had my car (and other) insurance with... didn't call. My sister-in-law (my wife's sister) who sells insurance... didn't call.... even though I mentioned several times at family dinners that we needed life insurance.

Eventually, the day came when I went online to buy a million dollars in life insurance. I was filling out the application..... and a guy walked in my front door (of the store, not my home), and said "I'm from New York Life. I was just in the area. Who do you have your life insurance with?" I said "You!". I'm sure it was the biggest sale he ever made. Cold calling does work.

When I was selling in home, the first several years I did the same thing. I went door-to-door and asked "If I give you a cutlery set (I showed it to them), would you let me demonstrate my vacuum cleaner?" Honest, that's what I said. I was looking for that *one person* a day that would let me talk to them. I made money that way, but I had an unlimited number of prospects. There was no *one person* I wanted to talk to. Anyone would do.

The flaw in this method was that I would talk to

anyone who would listen. Some people had no job, bad credit, a new vacuum cleaner, or any one of a number of reasons that made them bad prospects and made a sale highly unlikely. But the sheer volume of work I did, allowed me to make a good living.

After several years of doing this, I started asking qualifying questions to see if I really wanted to invest my time with them. That way, I didn't waste my time with people who could not buy... even if they wanted to. My sales shot up, because my time was better invested. And a side benefit of asking qualifying questions was that they actually wanted to see what I had..... because not *everyone* could get it.

My last several years of selling in people's homes, I worked almost entirely from referrals from my customers (I never ask for referrals from non-buyers), selling new machines to past customers. I also prospected lists of buyers of other high end products sold in people's homes.

Think about that last sentence. "...other buyers of high end products sold in people's homes". How can you use that?

Who has a very high chance of buying advertising from you? Someone who has bought lots of advertising from someone else. So you look in the Yellow Pages, look in the newspaper, make sure you call everyone that was in the Val-Pak envelope. It is far easier to sell advertising to someone used to buying advertising. They are usually already believers.

If you are brand new to selling advertising;
A quick tip; Go with an experienced rep for a few days. Just ride along. Don't talk when they are in front of a prospect. This benefits you both. You will see that cold calling is easy, and that nothing bad happens when you do it. Or you will see that you simply hate it, and would rather go to the dentist than talk to a new prospect. Either way, you'll be ahead. It benefits the person you are going with, in that they are now *forced to work*. It's amazing how much you will accomplish when someone is watching.... even when that someone is a new rep.

Good News & Bad News.
First the bad news. Your prospect is getting phone calls from telemarketers several times a day. When I'm in the store, I get between 15 and 30 calls a day from reps of every sort. Most are either selling internet Yellow Page advertising or wanting to

change my long distance, credit card processing, or utilities. Two or three times a day, a rep comes through the door selling something. This happens every day to everyone you want to talk to. These callers and visitors all have something in common. *I don't want to talk to them.* None of them give me an immediate reason to stop doing what I'm doing and listen to them. None of them make me *glad* to see them.

I haven't scared you away from cold calling? Good. Just don't do it the way *they* do it.
There's a better way.

How can you make the prospect glad to see you? Give them something they *want*, or tell them something they *want to hear*.

Here's a cold calling phone script that will get you in the door more times than not. "I saw your ad in the (Yellow Pages/newspaper/direct mail piece/etc.). It's a pretty good ad, and I work with local businesses to improve their advertising and reduce their costs. I think I can improve your ad results. I can show you what I mean in just a few minutes. Are you going to be in tomorrow at 3:00?" I used to use that script when I first started helping people write ads (I don't do it anymore). It really got phenomenal results.

Look at that again. You gave two benefits (improve ad & reduce costs), appealed to his vanity (It's a good ad). You need to say "*Show* you what I mean" ...not "tell you". If you say "*tell yo*u" the prospect will simply say "Tell me now".

What helps is that you are talking about a display ad. You really *have* to show him, not tell him.

The power of gifting.
Reciprocity is a powerful force. If you do someone a favor, or give them a gift, it's very hard for most people not to return the favor. For example, in my retail store I give free service on minor repairs. I will install a belt on a customer's vacuum cleaner.. and not charge for it. Why? Because I've tested the results, and found that for every dollar I spend in "free belts", I get back $60 in new vacuum cleaner sales. Some people just can't stand it when they don't return a favor. It eats at them. So they come back and buy from you... or buy before they leave.

When I was selling in people's homes I made it a policy that, if they sold a small item... or their kids were selling something for school, I would buy it... maybe multiples. My selling average skyrocketed in those cases. In fact, I don't remember a single case where they didn't buy from me after I bought from them.

So what's a good free gift when you are selling advertising? A fruit basket, a box of donuts, a book on advertising (Hint Hint), articles about what other businesses are doing to increase business, free tickets to a seminar, anything that would be considered a gift. Don't give gifts for *buying* advertising. That's a mistake, and could even be illegal. But delivering a small gift when you meet someone? Smart. And you'll be the only rep who did.

The Grapefruit Story;
When we first opened our store, we had a nice lady bring in a giant grapefruit. It was huge. She said that she was an attorney, and had extra grapefruit. She handed us one (with her card) and left. A year later she did the same thing... and the next year. On the third year, we called her to rewrite our will. We wouldn't have considered anyone else. By now, she was a *friend*. We have given her thousands of dollars and she has given us seven grapefruit. And we couldn't be happier.

Does this mean I'm suggesting you have to wait years to ask someone to buy? Of course not. She could have started the conversation of what she could do for us on the first visit... with the first grapefruit. But we didn't need a lawyer then. But everyone needs a lawyer *eventually*..... and we wouldn't have dared use anyone else. I really like grapefruit.

You have a huge advantage over the lawyer. Everyone you talk to needs what you have... *now*.

New Businesses Are The Pot Of Gold At The End Of The Rainbow.

You always want to get to owners of new business right away.... before they are even open to the public. Usually, they haven't committed to any advertising, their attitude is great (about advertising), you have a great reason to see them (Grand Opening), and they will get great results from practically any ads they run. And.. believe it or not... these are usually eager buyers of advertising. While you are looking for them... they are looking for *you*.

You want to get there fast... and *first*. The reason you want to be the first ad rep talking to them is this; Other ad reps may try to sell *against* your type of advertising. They may convince the new guy that they *only* need to advertise on TV (for example), and that all other media is a waste of money. They may have signed the business owner to a *huge* monthly contract that will be hard for the business owner to justify supplementing. So you want to get there first. You can get lists of people who just bought vender's permits (sometimes the local paper lists them). You can buy mailing lists of businesses that have just turned on the utilities (maybe the fastest way to get the name). You can also just stay on the lookout (by driving by) for new stores that are in the process of getting ready to open. You can get the lists from list brokers online, or just go to www.infousa.com. They have new business lists.

An Absolutely Guaranteed Way To Get To See 80% Of Your "Must Have" Clients.

I have used this method to sell to the very same business owners that you are selling to. It's a series of "While You Were Out" pink memo pad slips.

They are mailed to your prospect in a series of four mailings (one at a time, you choose the frequency) The first "While You Were Out" pink note is the size of a postcard. They get progressively bigger with each note. The last one the prospect gets is a whopping 2 feet by 3 feet. The message can be different each time.

It is virtually impossible to ignore these mailings. Your cost is about $10 for the whole series. The last note they get is in a cardboard tube. If they don't call after they get the last note, call them. In the last year I've used these "While You Were Out" message pad notes, over 80% of the CEO's either called me (usually after the biggest one), or talked to me after I called them. You can find out more by talking to the owner, Jeff Dettmer at www.outrageousmarketingproducts.com

If you've seen the new business written up in the paper....

I've done this method with near 100% chance of seeing the owner, having them glad to see me, and willing to listen to what I have to say.

I used to cut out of the paper, any story of a small business opening up, expanding, donating money, or having an employee (or owner's child) receive an award. Then I had the paper laminated at the local printer. It cost a few dollars. You can also buy frames, or have them mounted on plaques. Believe me, this works. You just walk in and say "I have a gift to deliver to Mr. ___". Do not give it to someone else to give to him (or her). Leave & come back if necessary. Very powerful technique. You'll be the only rep that did this. You just can't make a gift that's more specific to them and personal.

Once they have talked to you, whether they are a client or not, you know what business they are in, and maybe what interests them. If you see a newspaper story that applies to their business, or to them personally, cut it out and mail it to them with a short note attached. Do you want to be the "Go To Guy"? (or girl)? This is one way.

There is a danger in this "being a nice guy". Eventually you'll run into someone who will take advantage of you.. The way you can tell, is if they start asking you for favors beyond what you have done for them. For example, you give them a free ad. Then you call them to ask how the ad worked, and they ask you for another free ad. Don't do it. It will happen very rarely, unless you are seeing the worst quality people to begin with. It happens in all businesses. Just disconnect yourself from that person. They won't change.

Taking a survey. The wrong way and the right way.

If you read books on selling, you'll see this as a techniques. You walk in and say "I'm taking a marketing survey, may I get your answers to a few questions?". I've tried it with little success.

Why? Because you are opening the conversation talking about you... about what you need. That's a mistake. Nobody cares about you, until they see how wonderful you are.

This works; "Hi, Mr.____. I'm from the ____ company. I'm not here to sell advertising. I was wondering if you could tell me about how you advertise & what you find works. Do you have a minute?". Now, I know this sounds like it's about you... but it's really about the business owner having the chance to show how much he knows (or doesn't know) and brag. There is also the opportunity to complain about other reps, the economy, and whatever he feels like. You are a captive audience for him. Believe me, he doesn't want to pass up this chance. Just listen to what he says. He'll tell you what he knows about advertising, what he likes in advertising, which product you offer would appeal to him, what products to avoid, and how to sell him. If it takes a half an hour, take it. Just don't let it continue down a road of "...and that's why my wife left me... now let's talk about my sore feet...".

If he starts going down a non-profitable train of thought, just wait for the end of a story and say "Wow, you sure lead an interesting life. A little bit ago you brought up a great point..." and just change the subject back to business. This first visit is to build rapport. After a business owner tells you all his troubles and brags about his accomplishments, it's amazing how *brilliant* he'll think you are.

Who to see first. Low Hanging fruit.
In every market there are people who are ready to buy. In advertising sales, these people buy advertising from almost anyone who sells it. They buy because:

> 1) They know how to make it work, and the more avenues in advertising, the better (this is rare).
>
> 2) They like advertising for ego reasons, or have a huge budget, and just want to spend the money.
>
> 3) They sell something with a high enough profit margin that almost any ads will generate a profit.

Whatever their motivation, these people buy lots of advertising. The easiest way to find them is simply to look at ads in the local newspaper, direct mail magazine or envelope, and the Yellow Pages. You may as well start your sales career off with a bang. See these people first.

But you need to know this; Just because they spend money on advertising, doesn't mean they know *how* to advertise. Most companies don't track their ad results. They don't really know which ad is working and which ad is *not*. After you ask them "Is this ad working for you?" in reference to an ad they are already running... ask "How do you know?". The answer to that question will tell you whether they really know if it's working or not.

If they are compulsive advertising buyers, my advice is to accept the business, try to give them information and suggestions to make the ad better, and let it go.

What if they won't kiss on the first date? (Did that get your attention?)
Everyone buys at their own speed. Different people make decisions at different speeds. There is a *sales process timeline*. You want your client closer to the end of the process *before* you sell the advertising. You want to keep communication going between you. This can be done with mail, E-Mail, recorded message, or touching base by phone.

Even if they bought the first day, the sales process continues. You are in the relationship business... the results business. The first sale you make *supports* the second sale... which *supports* the third sale. That's why selling gets easier with the same client.

The ultimate inducement (a free ad).
Have you ever pulled into a restaurant's parking

lot... and it was empty? What did you think? Did you leave? Many do. An empty parking lot pretty much screams "Nobody eats here!"

Next to our retail store was a group of 50 telemarketers. We told several of them that they could park in front of our store. Why? Because it looked like we were *busy*. It looked like *something was happening* at our store. If you sell direct mail or newspaper advertising, it helps if your clients see lots of other ads. The consumer won't notice and won't care.... but it looks good to a client.

Do you use filler public service ads? I have a better idea. Either barter to sell the space or give it away to a new prospect. Make it *work* for them. It's very hard to say "No" to an offer for a free ad. And it's *impossible* to say "No" to the next ad, after the first one creates a profit.

I owe my living to my ad rep. The Legend Of Blaine Drake.

After selling in people's homes for 20 years, I decided to open my own retail store. For the first two years we made a living, because I knew how to sell. But our store wasn't growing. We tried advertising on radio, cable TV, and by direct mail. We tried every weird, off the wall advertising you could think of. No ads worked. I gave up on advertising.

One day, this short young man with a smile ear to ear.... came into my store and politely waited for me to finish selling a vacuum cleaner. He watched what I was doing and didn't interrupt me until the people left (Never interrupt a sales situation). He sold advertising for a direct mail coupon book called The Town Money Saver. I was polite (because he was polite) and said "No. We tried direct mail... *and it doesn't work*."

His name was Blaine. He quietly asked me several questions about how I sold (asking how we do something is a form of *compliment*). It was hard not to like him, but my mind was still closed. Then Blaine said those magic words "What if I gave you an ad for free. No obligation. Just to see if we can make it work". Try saying "No" to that!

Of course, I accepted. And the ad bombed. The next month, Blaine offered me another free ad. He would spend 20 minutes asking me questions, and *listening to the answers*. (that's another huge compliment... actually listening). I insisted on paying for the ad.... and by now, I looked forward to his visits. But the ads were a waste.

So I actually did something that almost no advertiser does. I bought a book on advertising. Then another. I studied ads that repeated themselves (I figured they must work, if they are repeated).

I went to a seminar... then another. In one month, I spent over $3,000 on books, tapes (this was before CDs), and seminars. (My wife was *not* happy... we didn't really have $3,000 that month to waste). I studied advertising for several months... all the time trying new ways to advertise my vacuum cleaners. Years later, my library was now way over 1,000 books. Almost all are on advertising, marketing, and sales.

Then one month my ad produced a profit. Then a bigger profit. I figured out what part of the ads were making the sale, and what parts were wasted. My ad size went from a half page to a full page. Then two pages... then three (All different offers).

My ads were paying me up to 40 times their cost in net profits, with a seven year average of 8 times their cost. People in my industry started asking me to help them with their ads.

I was happy, and creating wealth from my store. Blaine was happy.. I was his biggest advertiser... and the best result of all this was..... I discovered that you really can make ads pay off... in different media.

Blaine never learned how to advertise. It didn't occur to either one of us (at the time) that this was something for him to learn. But he made me *want* to advertise. He made me *want* to make it work. We became friends. This went on for several years.

Then I got the call from his office. Blaine had fallen off his roof and died. I was the first client they called. He never asked me for a favor, always did what he promised, and was one of the most genuinely nice people I ever met. If not for Blaine, I never would have studied advertising, wouldn't be giving seminars, and wouldn't be writing this. I owe him.

Blaine gave me a free ad. Had he not done that, I wouldn't have started advertising with him. And then I wouldn't have continued to buy multiple pages for several years. I have no idea if Blaine was just being a nice guy when he gave me that first free ad, or if he thought of it as a marketing technique.... and I never asked. But it sure paid off.

Referrals

Master this art, and your sales will explode!
The single best prospect is an established customer that has been doing business with you for years. The *second* best prospect is someone who is told by that "very happy client" that they should do business with you, or at least listen to what you have to say.

The majority of selling is getting the client to *like* you, *trust* what you say, and have *evidence* that what you are selling is good for them. A referral from a satisfied customer gives you all these things.

One note; Wait to ask for referrals until your client is very satisfied with your work, and the results. Don't ask for referrals at the first meeting. They will not be strong referrals. Wait until the client has talked to the referral. You need to be a "Friend of a friend" for this to be completely effective. This may actually take a few months into the relationship. And I don't ask for referrals from unsatisfied clients (Yes, you'll still get them.) Or from prospects that didn't buy. I only want to contact referrals from happy motivated clients.

We are going to talk about the best ways to get a referral in a minute.

Here's how to **not** *ask* for a referral: "Do you know of anyone who might be interested in advertising with me?". Even the most enthusiastic client will say "Wow, not off the top of my head, but I'll let you know if one comes to mind". And you have nothing.

The way to **not** *call* a referral is this: "Hello, Mr.___? This is Bob with the newspaper. I just talked to your friend Bill, and he thought you might be interested in running an ad, are you?". He will say "No" and you will have lost him as a prospect.

I have a method to get referrals and contact the referrals. It's devastatingly effective.

First, Getting Referrals:

"Bill, what kind of job have I done for you?" (They applaud you for their results working with you).

"Bill, I work mostly by referral. What other business owner locally *have you told* about your results?"

"And what did they say?"

"Would they appreciate a free look at their advertising, to see if I could be of help?"

"What's their phone number?"

"*Who else* have you told?"

"What did *they* say?"

"Who are you close friends with that owns a local business?" "Have you talked about advertising?"

"Who has given *your* name as a referral before?"

Of course, you wait for the answers before you ask the next question.

What you want are just four or five high quality referrals. But we are not done. Now that you have the names, you ask:

"If you were me, who would you call *first* on this list?" "Why?"

"Is there anyone on this list that I really shouldn't talk to, right now?"

"The best referral you gave me is Joe. Is Joe at his business right now? May I borrow your phone for a second?"

(Or "May I call him right now, in front of you?")

The only reason you want to use the client's phone, is that the person you call may have Caller ID. If you call from your phone, they may not pick up the phone. But if you call from the *client's* phone... they *will*. It isn't necessary to use the client's phone, but you'll get through more often.

And you call Joe. Right there, in front of Bill. Do it. You'll get an entirely different reaction from Joe than if you waited and called by yourself. If you call & get a gatekeeper (secretary, assistant, mother) hand the phone to Bill and have *him* ask for Joe.

If you get Joe, just say "Hi, this is Claude with ABC Advertising. I'm sitting here with your friend Bill.. Say 'Hi' Bill (Bill says 'Hi' into the phone). Anyway, I've done some work with Bill to save money on his advertising and make it more profitable (or whatever benefit Bill got from you). I have no way of knowing if I can really be of service to you... but I promised Bill that I would *at least show you* what we do. Would you have 15 minutes today or tomorrow? I promise not to take longer than that."

This referral script is so effective that I've had several clients ask me to teach it to their reps.... after I called the prospect from their office. There are several reasons that this approach works so well. Let's go over it step-by-step. There are reasons for every part of it.

"Bill, what kind of job have I done for you?" (They applaud you for their results working with you).
You want Joe to say something positive, it makes it easier and more natural now to ask a little favor.

"Bill, I work mostly by referral. What other business owner locally have you told about your results? And what did they say? Would they appreciate a free look at their advertising, to see if I could be of help?"

Referrals are *much* stronger if the client has already talked to them. And it narrows the universe of people that the client has to think of when you ask for names. You may only get one name, you may get four. Never just ask "Who do you know that I could call?" The client will then have to think of everyone they know, and they will blow you off.

"What's their phone number?"

I have a legal pad out. I have it out before I start talking about referrals. You can use a form if you like, but only have room on it for a few names. If you ask 20 questions about each name, and the client sees that there is room for twenty names, you'll be politely told "I'll get back to you. I can't think of anyone right now."

This needs to feel like a five minute discussion to the client. Getting the names really will only take ten minutes or so.

"Who else have you told? What did they say?"

You only want a few highly qualified names here. You can always go back for more names after you see the few names you'll get here.

You want to know what the referral said (if they said anything) so you'll know the best approach when you meet them. Also, if the client says "Paul said I was a moron for buying from you. They said they can get the same advertising for half the rate through a media buyer". ..Don't you want to *know* that? And if your client says "Paul said that he was thinking of trying the same thing, and asked for your phone number." ...Don't you want to know *that*?

"Who are you close friends with that own a local business? Have you talked about advertising?"
This is just adding a source of more names. You really want to know if they have talked about advertising. If they have, it's a stronger referral. If they have discussed you and your company, it's a *much* stronger referral.

"Who has given *your* name as a referral before?"
This is actually slightly humorous. It's like they are "returning the favor". It may add a name or two. And the referral will *have* to see you, just to return the "favor" to the client.

"If you were me, who would you call first on this list? Why?"
You want to call the best referral *first*. Also, you want to know *why*. You'll pick up some pretty good information by asking. If the client says "I'd go see Paul first, because he said he was looking to advertise more very soon. He just got in a new line of motorcycle helmets in, and wants to promote them", don't you want to know that? Also, you don't want Bill hearing a bad call right away. You want Bill hearing a good call that goes smoothly. Because you want Bill to keep giving you names later.

"Is there anyone on this list that I really shouldn't talk to, right now?"
Now, why would you ask that? Because he might say "Yeah, Barry is going through a mean divorce right now. And his mind isn't on business. I'd call him in a few months". And if you call Barry, and he blows you off, it's harder to make a good first impression... the second time you call.

"The best referral you gave me is Gary. Is Gary at his business right now? May I borrow your phone for a second?" (Or "May I call him right now, in front of you?")
OK, I admit.. I know you may be shaking a little

right now. And it does take just a wee bit of nerve to call in front of the client. But it will double the number of referrals that actually see you.

Why? Because if you are sitting right in front of the client, the person you're calling can't say "No" to you... and then tell Bill a completely different story. Plus, it's far harder to say "No" to you when Bill is in the room. He's essentially saying "No" to Bill. It's a very strong technique. After you do it once or twice, you'll never want to do it any other way. It's that good.

If you get Joe, just say "Hi, this is Claude with ABC Advertising. I'm sitting here with your friend Bill.. Say 'Hi' Bill (Joe says 'Hi' into the phone). Anyway, I've done some work with Bill to save money on his advertising and make it more profitable (or whatever benefit Bob got from you). I have no way of knowing if I can really be of service to you... *but* **I** *promised* **Bill that I would at least show you what we do. Would you have 15 minutes today or tomorrow? I promise not to take longer than that."**
You *have* to say you are with Bill. He *has* to say "Hi" so that Bob knows that you are telling the truth, and that he's.... well.... *trapped* into talking to you.

You say **"I have no way of knowing if I can really be of service to you..."** because it lessens the implied commitment on Joe. It makes it a little easier to say "Yes" to the appointment.

"....but I *promised Bill* that I would at least *show you* what we do."
Wow. Now Joe can't say "No" without saying "No" to Bill. The appointment is now a *favor* to Joe that can't be refused (almost never, anyway). "show you" is important, because if you say "tell you" then Joe can say "Well, tell me now... now that you have me on the phone" ...and you have just been handed an anchor while treading water.

That's pretty much it. If they kiss you off after *this*, they weren't prospects to begin with.

If your client says "You can call them, but don't mention my name" ..don't bother. Something is wrong. Just thank them for the names, and drop the matter.

Now, I understand that you may still refuse to call referrals from the client's office. I understand. If you haven't done it before, some reps will be uncomfortable. There may also be reasons you just *can't* do it. The client gets interrupted, he gets called away.... whatever. Just be sure you don't lie to yourself about why you don't want to call from the client's office. It isn't because the method doesn't work.

So here's how you call the referral after you leave the client's office;

"Hello, Don? This is Claude from the ABC advertising company, I was just talking to Jake Smith over at Kittens Inc. Jake gave me your name as a referral, and *I promised Jake I'd at least show you* how we save you money on your advertising. I don't know if my service is right for you, but we can tell after a quick look at what we have. Ten minutes, and I'll be out of your hair. May I stop by tomorrow?"

Now, say it all in one long run-on sentence. If you stop for a second, it's *way too easy* for Don to ask a question like "Can you just mail me the information?". That's bad. You want Don to feel like saying "No" to you is the same as saying "No" to Jake.

This method is less effective than calling from the referrer's phone..... but it works for me about 50% of the time. Of course, once you are in front of Don, you can take as long as *he* likes.

I used to get the question "How long will this take?" My answer was "Ten minutes, unless you have questions". It's hard to say "No" to ten minutes, and they always ask questions.

"But Claude, if this system for getting referrals is so great, why still cold call?"
You need to get established clients to get referrals *from*. So for the first several months, at least, that's what you'll be doing. I still cold call, although most of my business is now referral and people seeking me out.

After you have been getting referrals for several months, you will notice a phenomenon; Some clients give you great referrals, and some give you bad referrals... or none at all.

If they give you great referrals... you go back for *more*. Eventually you are only working client referrals that are high quality prospects. I always send a gift (or at least a Thank You card) after I see the referrals given. And I always let the referrer know how the conversation went. If you don't call to tell the referrer what happened, he'll have to find out from the referred person. At a bare minimum, you need to call the referrer. He will stop giving you referrals if you stop giving him feedback.

When prospecting please.. don't do *this*.

I get calls from radio stations occasionally that say "I have made up an ad for your store, may I play it for you?". The answer is always "No". Here's why, the prospect (a smart one anyway) hates that. You don't know me. You don't know what appeals work, what products I sell, my strong or weak points... anything about me. *But you think you have an ad that's going to bring in customers?*... without ever talking to me? And the fact that you spent time creating the ad... before you ever contacted me... doesn't make me feel obligated in the least. I get the same thing from print salesman; "I wrote this ad for you, may I show it to you?". No.

What I would be eager to get is "several ads from people *in your business* that we have seen *work*. May I drop them off?". Absolutely! Just make sure the ads are not from a local competitor. Another approach would be; "I saw your ad, and think I can improve it". At least they saw my ad.

A Great Couple Of Questions To Ask To Get Them Focused On Wanting To Advertise.

"How many people in your area buy what you sell on average... every day?"

"After they figure that out (you take the population, divided by the years it takes between purchases, divided by 365... got that?). A wild guess on their part will do fine. Let's say they say "Ten a day".

You say "How many of those ten are you getting right now?"

Then "How many, out of those ten, would you like?"

"Let's see how we can help you get those, shall we?"

The Value Of One Additional Client

Sometimes it may feel like you are going through too much trouble to get a client. Let's do the math and see if it's worth the trouble.

Your commissions are going to vary wildly depending on the media, monthly contract, and length of your business relationship with the client.

But let's be very conservative. Let's say that your client earns you $200 a month in commissions. You keep that relationship for ten years.. before the client moves, dies, or goes out of business.

That's $2,400 a year in earnings... $24,000 over ten years.

To earn that same return, you would have to invest $48,000 at a rate of 5% return (Good luck finding that!).

So each client is effectively worth $48,000 to you.... each client.

And every client gives you referrals that are very easy to sell.

The clients themselves take little work after you design the initial offer for them.

What would you be willing to do to find a $48,000 treasure?

Additional Ways To Get That First Ad Sale.

Barter:
Do you want to practically guarantee that a business owner will buy an ad? Barter the price of the first ad for something they sell. Make sure it's something you either would have bought anyway, or something you can sell quickly on E-Bay. It also works, although to a lesser degree, if you barter *half* the cost of the first ad. Only do this on the first ad... and make sure that ad produces.

(To find out how to do *that*... read my book **The Unfair Advantage Small Business Advertising Manual**). Make sure the advertiser understands that you are bartering only on the first ad. If you do it on the second ad, you have trained the advertiser to *only* take an ad from you if you barter.

Barter with other media.
You can barter your ad space (or radio time, TV time, etc) with other media. I would contact the advertising sales manager. If you sell direct mail advertising, simply ask the newspaper sales manager if you would like them to put an ad in your media for ad space in their newspaper... then you advertise in the newspaper for your ad sales. The trick is to advertise something the advertiser gets other than just ads. My mentor Dan Kennedy calls this a "widget". I would advertise for "a free report on **The Seven Mistakes Advertisers Make That Are Costing Them A Fortune**". With your phone number. You deliver the report (after you write one, of course), and discuss advertising. Nobody would want to know about advertising mistakes unless they were thinking about advertising, right? Your report could be 5-7 pages long and have most of your sales arguments in it. Of course, the purpose is not to mail or drop off a report. The report is just a

way to get to talk to the owner. You may only get a few calls a month off of such an ad... but they will be very high quality leads.

Show examples of successful ads.
When seeing prospects, after they agree to buying an ad (or a run of ads) from you, Show them a few examples of ads *you've helped advertisers on*. You want the advertiser to start seeing you as an advisor, not an ad rep. If you don't show that your input helps the ads generate more profit, they won't listen.

Have a website and promote it.
I'm assuming that you work with a company that has a website. It also needs to be listed in the local search engines, and the client has to be able to contact you. Your business card should always list the website. It acts like an expanded brochure.

Your business card.
Your company may provide them. Here's the problem; regular business cards don't *sell*.
Make a list of all the reasons that a business would advertise with you. Now pick out the top six or eight. Use these on your cards as bullet points. My cards are fold over... meaning that there is four sides. The bullet points go inside. When you give

anyone your card, *present* it to them.

"Here is how to get a hold of me, (open it up) and here are the top six reasons business owners advertise with me. (Show the back of the card) and here is what one of my clients said."

On the back of the card have a testimonial that talks about *results*. Not "John is a great guy".. but "*John placed an ad that cost me $675, and it generated $12,978 in profits! Let's do it again!* -Bill Cline, Owner of Cline's Motorcycles"

If you don't have a testimonial yet, any testimonial like that from your company will do.

The Best Way To Build Your Business

The power of first impressions
When I was selling in people's homes, we had a group of people we didn't want to see.... Teachers. Now don't misunderstand, I like teachers. Some of my friends are teachers, Some of my best customers are teachers. But when you are selling in the home, you have about an hour or two to take them through the entire decision making process. Teachers tend to be more analytical than most, and like to do research before they buy. This is actually the

smartest way to buy, and I respect that. But when you're selling in their home, you are looking for a quick decision.

In retail it's completely different. There is no time constraint. Teachers can see your ads, do research online, shop other stores, and gather information. *Then* they come in your store. Most of the buying process has been done before they ever see you. We all buy at different speeds.... but what they need before they buy is pretty much the same;

> 1) They like you, think you have something that may help them, and will listen to you.
>
> 2) They have confidence that you are looking out for their best interests. They trust you.
>
> 3) They believe that what you have will work for *them*.
>
> 4) They are confident that the risk of making a bad decision is minimal.... or non-existent.

These are not steps that occur in order. They may happen all at once, or in a different order. But they all need to happen. Because selling advertising is largely a business of relationships, you need to sell at their speed, not yours. That's why whenever you visit them, you offer them a gift, information, brochures, invitations, etc. You need a reason to show up. "I was in the area" doesn't sound as good as "I thought you might find this interesting". Eventually most will buy.

How do you know when to stop this "courting process"?

In every visit, they are either *more* excited to see you or *less*. They are either closer to buying or further away than they were on the visit before. When you sense that they are moving away from buying... I just wouldn't show up again. A few may call you and buy, but your time is better invested in trees bearing fruit.

One of the huge benefits of hosting an advertising seminar is that they will go through those buying factors, at the seminar, before you even talk to them about advertising. We'll discuss how to do that later.

"You can get everything in life you want, as long as you get enough other people get what they want"

-Zig Ziglar

How To Absolutely Beat Your Competition

Don't compete. This is not an either/or situation. If you sell newspaper advertising, radio advertising actually helps the newspaper results. If you sell radio advertising, direct mail actually helps your results. All effective advertising builds consumer awareness and demand for the product. The more advertising done (in different media) the better the total result.

Have you ever seen an infomercial? Did you know that, if that same item is sold in Big Box Stores, that it *increases* the infomercial sales? Did you know that infomercials actually increase the retail sales? Reps that sell other advertising media aren't your competitors... they are your colleagues. And the client should advertise in every way that *works*, not just your method..

Your real competition is ignorance of your market. Most advertisers simply don't see how your media will make them a profit, and don't want to go through the hassle of learning more about what you offer. You win by building a relationship, showing that "knowing you has value", educating your clients to better methods (tactfully... oh, so tactfully!), and showing profitable results from advertising with you.

Now from a buyer's point-of-view; Do you want to completely turn off a prospect? Complain about the other reps out there. Complain about your manager. Complain about how hard it is to get business. Spread a rumor about another rep... or advertiser. Your prospect may laugh with you... but after you leave, you have been written off as a someone to avoid. I mean it.

You can let your *client* go on and on about what a moron his competitor is (or your competitor).

But if you even just *agree* with him.... he'll tell people *you said* it. It's happened to me.

"Sure, give a man a fish; you feed him for a day. Teach a man to fish; you feed him for a lifetime. But most people really just want a steady supply of fish"

-Claude Whitacre

"Selling Is A Numbers Game"?

If you've been selling for more than five minutes, you've heard this. The more people you see, the more you sell. True enough. But have you ever gone home after a hard day of beating the bushes, without a sale? We all have. Does your spouse want to hear "Honey, it's a numbers game. We'll get the next one"? No. She (or he) may say it to *you*, because they love you. But it isn't what they are thinking. When I was selling in people's home, I didn't care about this being a numbers game. I cared about making *this* sale.. to *this* prospect. *Now*.

I'm going to take off my "author hat" for a minute and talk to you as one salesperson to another.

I mean this from my heart; The prospecting methods I tell you about *work*. The qualification methods *work*. They are the Fast Track. They don't *take* time, they *save* you time.

When I first started selling in people's homes, I was terrible. After a few months I was earning a living through sheer hard work. Eventually I studied books on selling (there's a lot of bad advice out there), and I got better at selling. I learned from master salespeople. I tested new ideas, and saved the ones that worked. After every appointment I would analyze why they bought.. or why they didn't. The last few years I was selling in the home, I was closing a tad over 50% of the people I had just met (that invited me in their home) and over 90% of my referrals. I kept a journal of what I did. My last three years of selling, I had never gone an eight hour period of working without making a sale. What did I do?

I started every presentation finding out about the prospect. I listened. I asked questions that are almost identical to the qualifying questions I'm about to share with you. Spending several minutes (as long as the prospect needs) asking questions and listening, is the faster method of selling. Building rapport is faster than trying to just "sell ad space". The last several years I sold vacuum cleaners, I had a fellow distributor that wanted to learn how I was selling so many vacuums, at a higher price than she was.

She worked with me for a week. At the end of the week, she told me "Do you know the difference between us? I'll be done with my presentation in thirty minutes. You'll spend thirty minutes just asking questions, before you really get started. I'll do fifteen product demonstrations in a week, sell three, and think I'm on top of the world. You'll do six demonstrations in a week, sell five, and spend the rest of the week wondering why you missed that sixth one."

She was right, and we both had a laugh. But that's how you get *better*.

"But Claude, I sell to business people, isn't that different from selling to consumers?"

Only in a few ways. I would dress differently if I was selling in an office. I may tone down the humor a little. I may get to the point faster (after all, they *are* making a living there).

And there are products that you wouldn't sell at their place of work, and some products you wouldn't sell at their home.

But here is the core of it; The people you see are the same people whether you see them at their office or at home. They don't change. What appeals to a CEO at the job will appeal to him at home. He's the same guy. To you he may be the CEO of a large company... but to his in-laws, he's just the idiot that married their sister.

When I talk about giving gifts, and doing favors.... that doesn't mean that you act in a subservient way. You aren't their employee. You aren't the child "leaving an apple for the teacher". You are a fellow business person providing a professional courtesy. When I'm selling the idea of giving a speech, I talk in a conversational way, and always sound like an equal. I may tone down the humor (a few people just don't like it at all), but I always sound like a business associate on equal footing... a colleague.

A huge mistake I see is sending sales letters (or Thank You notes) that are formal, and sound institutional. It also happens when a small company wants to give the impression that they are a large company. They de-personalize the sales copy. They take all the personality and flavor out of the letter.

But did you know that huge companies are spending fortunes trying to look and sound like they are smaller companies, or even individuals? Why?

Because a "company" never reads your sales letter.... an individual person does. So, talk to that person in your sales message.

"Don't complain about the rules. Get better at the game"

-Claude's Dad

How To Think Like A Marketer

Most reps think like a salesperson. They think about making the next sale. So do I.

But a *marketer* thinks about more than that. A marketer considers the many ways to increase business. They think about how to make the sales process faster, and how to automate more of it.

(The prospecting, not the actual person-to-person selling).

Selling is the transference of *feeling*. Selling is a part of marketing. But Marketing includes everything that can be done to increase business and profitability.

For example, marketing includes (for your client);
Location of store, visibility of outdoor sign, how easy is the sign to read, is the sign lighted at night, indoor signage, price tags-and what they say to the shopper, the hours you are open, are the hours posted, are the hours in your ads, do you accept credit cards-which ones, are the credit cards listed in the ads, do you deliver-pick up, how bright is your store, do you use natural lighting, is the store neat & clean, are popular items easy to find, are the employees knowledgeable, are your pets in the store, is there an odor, do you smoke, do you chew tobacco (in the store), are your items priced competitively with your competition, are the items displayed according to price, are there store specials, are they advertised, is parking easy, are there parking spaces available, is the parking lot lighted, how are customers greeted, how fast are customers greeted, do you have a public bathroom, are there impulse items on the counters, which items, are they demonstrated, do you have a place for customers to sit down, what is your selection-

how large-how brightly lit-how attractive-in what order, do you do "special orders", do you service what you sell-what others sell, how long does service take, do you call customers when their part is in, do you lose your temper with customers, do you swear in front of customers, do you yell at employees in front of customers, do you wear a store branded shirt, who is next to you at your location, is your store stand alone or in a plaza, is the neighborhood getting better or worse, are there many closed stores near you, is there music playing in the store-how loud-what kind of music, what is the temperature of the store, where is your counter located, what is your reputation around town, do you close for lunch, do you have bad breath, do you show irritation with your customer's children, do you remember your customer's names, do you talk to customers when you see them outside the store, do you give refunds, do you honor warranties, is there graffiti anywhere at your location, are you funny-do you tell jokes-are they offensive, do you listen to customers, how do you handle complaints, what range in prices do you have, is your selection varied or concentrated on low end-high end, do you talk politics or religion with customers, do you have a political sign in your store, what bumper stickers do you have on your car, how do you answer the phone, do you have voicemail-what does it say, do you return calls quickly....

I could go on and on for several pages. Almost everything listed above is completely in the control of the client. All of this affects sales.

The same goes for *you*.
There are a thousand things you do, or don't do, that affect sales. Most of them are the same as the list I just gave you. Maybe you should read that list again.

I had a rep (I forget what he was selling) that smelled so badly from cigarette smoke that I cut him off after just a few minutes. I was getting a headache. I couldn't stand it, so I told him I wasn't interested. Maybe I really *was* interested... but I'll never know. I couldn't get past the smell.

"How can I make this sale?" is a question salespeople ask.

"How can I make prospects want to do business with me?" is what marketers ask. See the difference?

Great Advertising Will Not Overcome Bad Marketing - *Ever*

When clients send me ads to look over, I give them suggestions on how to improve the ads. I actually did a survey once of 100 clients that used ads I gave suggestions on. Seventy five told me that the ad at least doubled what it cost. If the ad cost $5, they netted at least $10. Usually lots more. Twenty five told me that the ad either didn't make a profit or made no money at all.

How can this *be*?

Well, after I asked the twenty five to show me that ad they ran, sixteen showed me an ad that either didn't follow my advice, or they *did* follow my advice but they changed something after I talked to them... or both. I'm not talking about minor changes in text, I mean they took out vital pieces, and added something they thought was cute.

The other nine clients did exactly what I suggested to the letter. Their ad still lost money.

Now, I didn't visit any of these people, so this is just a guess. Something in their marketing (or probably several things) kept the ads from working.

For example, I have a friend that opened a mattress store here in town. He advertised every few days in the local paper, His prices were at least 30% lower than any of his three competitors, his service was excellent, and he had a good selection. But every year, his sales shrank. Eventually he had to close his doors. Why? He *yelled* at his customers. He would argue with them about anything. Every day he would have someone vow never to come back in his store. Every day. Eventually word got around, and it killed his business.

No advertising could help him.

I tell you this for two reasons; Some clients will get bad results from any advertising they do, and there is nothing you can do about it. Fortunately, they are a small minority. The other reason I tell you this is that you can help your client with their marketing. As long as they will listen, and keep an open mind, I would keep trying.

"Everything is impossible, until someone does it"

-Unknown

How To Get Your Client To Think Like A Marketer

You can't make wholesale changes in the way your clients do business. But you can try to make it easier for them to see the profit in;

1) Tracking their ad response.

2) Thinking about Return On Investment in advertising, instead of advertising cost.

3) Learning how to effectively advertise.

4) How to get away from the "Ad Budget" mentality.

You can do this by repeatedly giving them articles that support what you are saying. The fastest way is by having them attend a seminar on advertising that covers these points.
At the risk of sounding like a self-serving capitalist... you could give them a copy of my book **The Unfair Advantage Small Business Advertising Manual**. All these points are covered in the book, and it's from an independent authority.

Qualifying Questions;

The Holy Grail

If there was *one* factor that increased my sales the *most*, it was asking qualifying questions.

There are several benefits to asking a series of questions like this. For example;

> 1) You come across as someone truly interested in them and their business.

> 2) You find out why they bought advertising before, and that can be the reason they buy from you.

3) You find out how much they know about advertising, and how easy they will be to work with.

4) You sound far more like an expert. These are questions experts ask, not clerks.

5) It gives you a chance to build stronger rapport.

6) Your recommendation of product will carry far more weight. They will feel like your recommendation is exactly fitting their situation.

7) You will stand out as unique. Almost never do I hear reps ask these questions.

Here are the questions;

- "What advertising do you do now?" (what media, how often)

- "What have you done in the past?"

- "What works best for you? Why do you think that is?"

- "What would you consider a successful ad?" People like to do two things; complain & brag. These questions allow them to fulfill those needs.

- "How much would your ad have to produce per dollar invested, before you would repeat the ad?"

That last question is designed to solicit the response "Anything over a dollar".

Repeat the question if you have to. Suggest an answer. "If your ad gave you back $1.50 for every dollar you invested in the ad, would you repeat the ad?"
This question also leads them away from the "We have an ad budget" response.

- "If we found out a way to increase your ads effectiveness, would you want to hear about it?"

That question allows you to now share information and give suggestions. Yes, it's a leading question. The first four questions are *discovery* questions. You just want to know the answer.

The last two questions are *leading* questions, designed to prompt a given response.

You can either just sell ad space, the same solution for everyone.... or you can ask questions, offer suggestions... and become an *advisor*. Your choice.

This was a very short chapter. But the single biggest difference between reps that are hugely successful, and ones that scrape by is this;

Successful reps ask qualifying questions, listen to the answers, and adapt their presentation to the client's specific situation. Poor reps *don't*.

Are You Selling A Contract For 13 Weeks, 12 Months, Or Any Other Bulk Sale (and you should)...Read *This*!

The reason ad reps sell contracts is because then the client is committed to a larger sale. That's the reason. You may hear from your manager (I hope not), that "The client can't expect a result from a single ad. They must advertise 13 times to be effective!". But this isn't true... even if they believe it. The answer is... it increases sales.

But can these ad runs be of benefit to the client? Absolutely!

Here's how. A 13 insertion (or the equivalent) order gives the advertiser 13 chances to make the ad profitable. You can even explain it that way. "We have a preferred rate for thirteen months. My suggestion *isn't* that you run the same ad for thirteen months, hoping it will start working. My idea is that we try an ad idea, and if it works... repeat it. If it isn't working, we need to tweak it, and measure the results of *that* ad. That gives us thirteen times at bat. And if the first one produces a profit, so much the better. But I'll stick with you until we can make it work to your satisfaction. Fair enough?".

When I started using radio advertising, the sales started coming in within 30 minutes of the first ad running. Had the ad not pulled right away (maybe after two days), I would have changed something, and waited for the result. The ad remained unchanged for several months.

The problem with most advertisers, if they only try one ad.. is that they try one ad.... not having a clue how to make an ad pay off... and the ad fails. Now they think that all advertising doesn't work. That's not true. The truth is, their *first attempt* at advertising failed.

So advertising runs *are* for the client's benefit, but because it gives them so many chances to get it right. And when you explain it *that* way, it will have a ring of truth to it, and won't sound completely self serving.

"Either write something worth reading or do something worth writing about"

-Benjamin Franklin

Advertising Media; Strengths & Weaknesses

Why do you care about other media? The more you know, the more you can help your client.
These are the best arguments I've heard from ad reps of these media. And they are all true.

Radio/Cable TV; When people are driving to work, most are still listening to the radio. At the beach, they aren't reading the newspaper. They are listening to the radio. At work, mostly the radio is on as background noise. With the radio, you can use voice inflection, which you can't do in print. You can create more excitement on the radio. You can test and compare ad results quickly using the radio. (But not as fast as online). You can use a proven talk radio host to plug your product. You can say "Mention this ad, and you will get a free __ with the purchase of a ___ ". That way, you can test whether the ad is working or not.. Most aren't going to hear your ad.

30 seconds VS a minute. A sixty second ad will outproduce a thirty second ad by several times, assuming you fill the time with reasons to buy. And a sixty second spot costs maybe 20% more than thirty seconds.
It also only takes a day or so to place your ad in rotation. So radio is useful in advertising events.

The bad news about radio: More people are listening to their CDs or IPods. And the listener has to be tuned into the specific station that you are advertising on... and you have to be listening at the exact time your ad is playing. I know that the ads play several times a day, but you still have to be there at the time they are playing. The radio station has to match your ideal customer. If you sell gardening equipment, advertising on a rap station probably won't pay off (because most middle aged people don't listen to rap). But advertising on a talk radio station with a conservative host might work.

Newspaper; Speed. You can run an ad tomorrow, if you like.. You can tell a lot in a large ad. And it's read by the more educated people. Older people also read the paper more than younger people.

Unfortunately, some newspapers are in trouble. Readership is down, the ads don't pull as well as they did five years ago.

Yellow Pages: The good news is that every business is listed in the Yellow Pages. Some people go there as the first place they look. And the people going to the Yellow Pages are very interested in buying, or they wouldn't have bothered.

The bad news is; Yellow Page readership is shrinking. More people are doing online searches more than ever, and the number is increasing. Plus, all your competitor's ads are right next to yours. Bad positioning.

Direct Mail; I don't mean individual letters with a stamp that you would mail out to everyone in your area. I mean "Marriage Mail". ADVO, Val-Pak, or any number of Shopper Magazines.

Here's a reality; Nobody goes out to their mailbox, takes their mail, and just throws it all away. If you use direct mail (especially postcards)...*everybody* will at least *see* the ad.

Everyone reads the mail. They can pick it up, put it down, look at it later, read it at 2:00 in the morning, and bring it in the store to check ad claims. And the cost per consumer is just a few cents. Of all the ways I've advertised, direct mail has consistently produced the highest returns, followed closely by radio.

The bad news about direct mail is just perception. Some advertisers call it "junk mail" and they won't use it because of that. I call it junk mail too. But call it what you will, almost every huge company uses it, and it's the most reliable way to advertise. The other downside is that you can't get the offer out right away. It may take a month to get the ad running. There is usually a schedule, sometimes monthly. But if your offer doesn't expire right away, it's a proven way to advertise.

If there are two or more direct mail ads being sent out the same month, make sure they are at least a week apart.

I know one direct mail company that purposely sends out their direct mail magazine two weeks after (or *before*, depending on how you look at it) their main direct mail competitor mails theirs. Smart. That way the results will not be diminished by readers getting two direct mail ads, from the same advertiser, at the same time.

Full page VS half page. (Or 30 seconds VS a minute)
I'm talking about direct mail ads and radio ads (although it applies to newspapers as well).
The headline will take up space at the top of the ad. Your contact information will take up space at the bottom of the ad. The amount of space these two things require doesn't change dramatically in different size ads. In a small ad, you have very little space to build value in what you are selling. In a full page ad, you may have four or five times the available "selling" space as in a half page ad. The more expensive the item you are promoting... the more this is needed. Bigger ads are also more visible and easier to find.

It's the same in radio ads. You can tell a whole lot more in a minute long ad than in a thirty second ad. A client called me and asked "How long should my ad be?" I said "Tell as much as you need to for the customer to want what you sell. Don't skimp...

don't pad. When you're done.. how long is *that*? Now you know how long your ad should be".

If you only need 30 seconds (of radio time) or 4 inches (of ad space) to tell the story, then that's great. But if it takes *more*, then you need a bigger ad.

One mistake some advertisers make is increasing the size of the ad by blowing up a smaller ad. Same ad, just bigger letters and pictures. This isn't the smart way. Your opportunity with a bigger ad is... you can build more value. You can tell more about the product, you can build more desire to buy the product. You have room to add more products.

Size matters.

How Big Should Be The Circulation/Broadcast Range?
In general, the higher the ticket price of the offer, the further the customer is willing to drive.
You may be willing to drive fifty miles to look at a car, but to buy a box of cereal? Not far.
You want the client to have the best "Bang for the buck". You may not like this suggestion, but I

would sell the ad space with more *local* circulation (if it's print), even if the prospect is willing to buy several areas... outside their local market. Why? Because the people closest to the advertiser are more likely to respond. And you want the first few ads to be *winners*. After the client has a few successes with you, *then* experiment with progressively farther away markets.

But if you sell a large market area, and the ad doesn't pay for itself, you may have lost the client.

Plus, suggesting the local market only, before expansion... shows the client that you are thinking of *them* instead of *yourself*. Very profitable.

"Advertising is only evil when it advertises evil things."

-David Ogilvy

The "Advertising Budget"

This is going to be the situation that you will face over and over again: "It's not in the budget" will be the reason the client will give you for not buying. When I was selling in the home I would hear "We may get laid off" or "I just got laid off" as the reason for not buying. It may have been true a few times, but it felt like I was personally causing half the population to get laid off from their job. Why would I hear this as a reason not to buy? Because it was something that happened to them *beyond their control*, that they could blame for not buying. It was simply easier and more painless than saying "I don't want to buy this from you".

If you are talking to the business *owner*, the ad budget they mention is.... *just made up*. They may have written it down somewhere, but it's just a figure that sounded good to them. There is absolutely no magic figure that is "the right amount". $500 a month? $30,000 a month, 5% of gross sales, 18% of gross sales..... are all figures they either read in a book, or heard from a friend. You can break them out of the "advertising budget" trap, after they understand the "Return On Investment" idea.... which we will discuss shortly.

"It's not in our budget" is a way to say "I'm not interested in this, but I want to be polite".

See? The "Budget" *won't let them* buy from you. They *want* to buy from you... but that darn budget is keeping them from it. That's the image they are trying to convey. But here's an even bigger problem. Many larger businesses *really have a budget*. This is true especially if they have someone in charge of the advertising who is not the owner. That person is *given* a budget to spend on advertising.

Your job... your mission... is to show the business owner that having an advertising budget is an absolute mistake. This will take five minutes with a few ...and several visits with most clients. But it is worth doing.

Here's the concept in a nutshell;
Ads either produce a net profit... or they produce a loss in profit. They are not an expense to be budgeted. Advertising is an *investment* that should pay off with a profit before they run the next ad. For example; If they buy an ad for $1,000... and that ad pays them back $3,000 within thirty days, what should they do next? Run it again! As often as possible. Would it make any sense to say "Well, Sure... that ad tripled our money, but we have an ad budget of $1,000 every three months. We'll have to wait for two more months."? That would be insane.

On the other hand, if you buy an ad for $1,000 and it produces no response at all, you wouldn't say "Well, this ad didn't work at all, but doggone it!.. we have that budget to spend. Go ahead and run it again". That would be equally as insane.

"The most powerful element in advertising is the truth."

-William Bernbach

Always Think "Return On Investment...ROI"

If you deposit $1 in the bank, it didn't *cost* you $1. You *invested* $1 (although at a minuscule return). If you put $1 in an account, and at the end of thirty day it grew to $3, would you ever say "That $1 wasn't in our budget. We can't afford to do this again"? Never. Any businessperson with a pulse would repeat the process adding as much money as they could... as long as they got the same return.

The same thing applies to advertising.

In fact, it would make sense to run multiple ads on multiple pages (three is my average). As long as every single page pays you a profit, why not?

But for any of the above arguments to take hold, your client needs to track their ad response. That means... *you* need to teach them how to do it, and why.

My other book (the one I keep yapping about) will explain this clearly to the client, if you can get them to read it. Seminars are the fastest way to change the way they see advertising though.

Tracking Ad Results. And How To Get Your Clients To Do The Same.

If you can show your client how to track their ad results, *and get them to do it* ...everything else will fall into place. The entire "ad budget" idea will vanish. They will be thinking "ROI" when thinking about ads, and you will become a favored advisor, because you showed them the best way to advertise.

I'm going to give you the easiest way to track ad response. You can do it with a computer program, but this is the easiest way. It's so easy, a computer illiterate business owner can do it. And they can get their employees to do it.

This is what you do. In their ads, have them put in an offer for something free (with purchase) if they bring in the ad. Have "Bring in this ad for a free ___with the purchase of a ___" so the advertiser will see evidence of the ad working. The problem usually isn't that the ads didn't work, it's that they *worked*, and the advertiser didn't *know* it.
With radio, you have the customer mention the ad when they come in to buy.

On the receipt, you have the person writing up the sale, simply write what ad they brought in. In the case of coupons (or even full page ads) you can keep a separate file, and simply place the coupons in a file, write the total of the sale at the top of the coupon, and add them up at the end of the month. Don't use "Bring in this ad for a free ___". People will come in for the free gift, and not buy anything.

You don't want the client adding "Zeros". You want the client adding dollars. If the customer doesn't come in with an ad or coupon, you simply ask at the counter "What caused you to come in today?" ...and write the answer at the top of the receipt.

The important thing here is to not prompt the answer. Believe me, if you ask "Did you see our ad on TV?", you'll hear a "Yes" about 80% of the time... even if you don't have an ad on TV.

In my store, I keep a chart that lists all the reasons they came in to buy; referral, a specific ad, saw our sign, past customer, etc. The "specific ad" section also lists the individual ads and the media they are in. At the end of the month, we just total these figures, and we know which ads worked, and which ads didn't. It's very easy for your clients to learn, and only takes a few minutes a day...After a few months of this experimentation two things will happen;

>1) Your client will get a real feel for what works and what doesn't.

>2) Virtually every ad they run will be generating a profit.

Won't *that* be a pleasant change?

"Advertising is the life of trade."

-Calvin Coolidge

What Is Total Customer Value (TCV)?

Your Big Gun.

Almost every business is a business of *relationships*. And relationships have a lifetime beyond the first sale. After the customer likes you, trusts you, knows where you are, and is used to giving you money.... they tend to *continue* giving you money. Usually this relationship last for several years... unless you do something to screw it up.

In direct mail and infomercials, they understand this concept very well.

Have you ever seen an infomercial? Have you ever bought from one?

You know that $39 course on "How to get rich on the internet"?

How much do you think that company paid in advertising to generate one $39 sale?
Maybe $200 or $300. I'm not kidding.

Why would they continue to advertise at such a loss? Because it isn't a loss.
The average customer that sends in that $39 will very quickly spend another $2,000-$3,000 with that company on other courses, websites, coaching, consulting, seminars, and will respond to constant upselling. The advertiser *knows the lifetime value* of their average customer.

The formula is easy; You simply ask your prospect...

"What is the average amount a new customer spends with you per year?"

"How many years does the average customer stay with you before they move on?"

Multiply the two figures, and you have your Total Customer Value.

As an example, let's say the client comes up with a figure of $5,000. The next question is "How much are you willing to pay to capture that $5,000 in business from each customer?"

If your single ad costs the client $1,000 and they will receive $5,000 in business from each new customer... how many new customers does each ad have to generate to be profitable? Less than one. And some of these customers *never* leave. So an ad that ran years ago will still be paying off today.

Sometimes you'll get a client that doesn't understand the math. They will say "I'll pay $500 to get that $5,000 profit." You can ask "Wouldn't you be willing to pay $4,000 to get back $5,000?". Of course, the answer is "Yes" (to any thinking person).

And the question "How many average new customers will we have to generate for the ad to be profitable?" is very powerful. I use a short form on the next page to show this formula. I leave it with the client. Eventually, he'll forget what you talked about, and forget the math. This will remind him *why* he's advertising with you.

And when you hear from a client "My business is word-of-mouth. We just keep growing, and we haven't advertised in three years!", you can remind them that the reason for this continued growth is from all the customers their ads generated *in the past*. And advertising now will just speed up that growth.

Here's a problem with this Total Customer Value argument. Even though it's absolutely true.... even though fortunes are made by taking advantage of TCV..... the client has to *wait* to see the total payoff from your ads. They may not want to wait. That's why you tell them about TCV... you mail them articles about TCV... you *remind* them about TCV... but you still work with them to make their ads pay off *now*.

Total Customer Value and Return On Investment Worksheet.

The value of *one* new customer

Average new customer purchase initially $_____

Average new customer purchases per year $_____

(After first year)
Number of years expected as a customer   X _____ (Dollar Amount Per Year)

Total New Customer Value = $_____

The formula is; Average customer purchases per year times average numbers of years plus initial sale equals Total New Customer Value.

Investment in recommended advertising Program.
$_____ per _____ ad/month/week

Total New Customer Value....divided by $_____

New Customer Acquisition Free

In this form, you'll find that the number of new customers an ad needs to generate is very low, many times less than one.

Think "Transaction Size"
How many sales does the merchant have to make to pay for your advertising recommendation?
If they sell homes, cars, water purifiers, furniture, windows, flooring, carpet, motorcycles, sports equipment, high end jewelry, chiropractic care, cosmetic surgery, or any product or service with a high transaction size... the answer will be *one*. It's easy to show a business owner how their ads will generate a profit for them when just one sale a month will pay for the entire ad recommendation. If they advertise and sell candy canes for a dollar... much harder.

Manage client expectations.
Is it possible that your client's ad will generate high profits the first time consumers see it? Sure.
But I wouldn't want my client *expecting* that.
High immediate profits are a bonus. They help cash flow. They are the goal of advertising (for you and your client).

But early on, mistakes will be made. You don't know everything about their business, and they know very little about advertising. So it usually takes several attempts to see immediate profits. This is the reason the client should commit to a contract. They need several attempts to find the right mix of headline, offer, price, and reasons to buy. So you need to explain that to the client.

My radio rep said it this way "Why don't we commit to six months. That way we'll have time to come up with ideas, test them, and find the ad format that works best for you. I'll stop by every couple of weeks to see if we need to make changes. Fair enough?"
My radio rep was a smart man.

Now in this case, my ads paid off right away. But I would have stayed with it for several months before I gave up... *because that was the plan from the start*.

Here's a common expectation...
"What percentage of people seeing my ad will buy? Isn't 2% standard?"
Prospects get an idea like this and they are setting themselves up for a *huge* disappointment.
The number of people seeing the ad is useful when comparing rates, but useless when comparing whether the ad is profitable or not. For example; I pay $650 for an ad that is mailed to 25,000 homes in my area. If 2% responded, that means 500 eager buyers would come in my store off the ad. Of course, that never happens.

I explained it to a fellow retailer once. She said "Claude, what kind of response do you get from your ads? I hear 2% is standard. I took marketing in college, and that's what I learned is a normal response rate".

I said; "Two percent is unrealistic. That 2% figure you hear about came from individually mailed sales letters to your customer list. I get an average response rate of one in *one thousand*. But so what? That still means I make 25 high end sales from every ad. So I am getting a *Return On Investment* of eight to one.... sometimes ten to one.. That's a home run *any* day. I would even continue the ads if I broke even. You know why? Because that means my new customers are being *acquired* at *no cost* to me. The ads are *paying* for it".

There really *are* businesspeople that shouldn't buy from you.
Let's assume you sell broadcast advertising. Radio/TV/Direct Mail... it doesn't matter. Let's say that everyone in your town will see or hear the ad. Is the businessperson selling a product or service that is used by many of the consumers in the area?

I had a customer come in my store, and I found out that they owned a local business. I asked what they sold. "Hospital gowns" is what he said. He told me that he saw my ads in the local direct mail book that was full of offers and coupons. He asked how well it worked. I said "Amazingly well. We get an average of a ten to one return on ad costs". He said "We tried it. We can't make it work for us."

I said "Do you sell to the public, or just to hospitals?".....He said "One local hospital and a clinic. We were hoping to get the two vets in town".

Claude the Evil said: "And so you mailed to 25,000 people that couldn't possibly want to buy from you? Why not just buy gifts for the two veterinarians... and deliver them with a sample gown?"
"It would have been cheaper" he nodded.

So you should stick to stores and businesses that sell to most people. Fortunately, that's most of the businesses out there.

"Nothing except the mint can make money without advertising."

-Thomas B. Macaulay

Answering Objections

Most of the time, you will get these objections at the *beginning* of the sales call. You may get them at the beginning, they may pop out when the prospect thinks of them during the sales call, they may come out at the end... although if you are doing your job, they *shouldn't* come out at the end. You should have answered them in the presentation.

This section is going to be radically different from anything you've read before. These won't be answers that sound good in print, or that *should* work. These are answers that will *really* work... because they address the objection from the client's point-of-view. Thinking of snappy comebacks and company generated patter doesn't sell. Actually answering the prospect's question in a way that *will make sense to the prospect..* sells. This will be the advanced training. Ready?

You should *never* get an objection *at the end* of your presentation.. Less than 10% of the time do I get a single objection to buying (in retail and in-home), when I suggest that they buy.. Getting an objection should be the exception, not the rule. Have you ever been to a doctor? They ask questions, you tell them about your pain, they ask more questions, and then they write you a prescription.
99% of the time, you pay them, pay for the prescription, and never question why this happened. *That's selling*.

You should follow this example. You trust your doctor and know that he's looking out for your best interests. (Maybe it's the white lab coat). Your clients should feel the same way about you.

You ask questions, find out how they feel.. about advertising, they ask you questions, and after you are both comfortable with the answers, you make a recommendation..... (write a prescription).

Have you ever heard an objection to buying? It's almost always (I'm being generous here) because the salesperson didn't answer the objection in the presentation. Objections are questions that weren't already answered. They are problems (in the prospect's mind) that are unresolved. If you had asked the qualifying questions, answered the prospect's questions completely, and managed the prospect's expectations.... there is no place for an objection to enter.

If you hear the same objection more than once a month, it's proof that you are ignoring the problem in your presentation. If you hear "It's not in the budget" at the end of your presentation, it's because you simply didn't show (to the client's satisfaction) that advertising is all about Return On Investment, and there shouldn't even *be* a budget.
The exception to this is if you are talking to an employee who can't make a decision, and must follow an employee manual.

If you are going to hear objections, it should be *at the very beginning* of the sales process.

Then you can answer them, and proceed.

One of the best reasons you ask qualifying questions is that they bring out objections... at the beginning of the process.

And here's what prospects *hate*... deferring the answer until later. Answer the question (or objection) as soon as it's brought up. Why? Because it's still what the prospect is thinking about the rest of the time you are there... until you answer the question. Here are a few of the more common objections that you will hear... and answers that will be convincing from a prospect's point-of-view.

"It's not in the budget"
"Of course not. If it were already in the budget, you would already be doing it, right?"

"Maybe you're spending *too much* money in advertising. May I ask you a few quick questions to see if I can help with a suggestion?"

"Just to help me in the future, what formula did you use to arrive at your budget?"

What you're doing with the first comment (it's not really a question) is to get them thinking outside of the memorized patter that they give to every advertising rep. You want to literally wake them up out of their train of thought. It's slightly risky, but if you smile while you say it, you'll get a little laugh... and they'll say "Well, I guess so", and they'll be listening closer to what you say next.

The second question really opens their eyes. Now they are all ears. No rep ever says that they may be spending too much in advertising. I've used this question in every type of sales situation.
It's *devastating.*

The third question gets them telling you the percentage of gross sales allocated to advertising. You want them telling you about their "budgeted advertising". The more they talk about it, the easier it is to get them thinking in your direction.

"How do you track your ads effectiveness to know if the ad is profitable?"
Now you'll find out that they don't track their ads at all. If they do track ads, this "ad budget" idea will dissolve quickly.

"If you found a way to advertise that produced $3 in net profits for every dollar invested in the ad, how would that affect your budget?"
You'll probably have to explain ROI to them, or at least how it affects advertising. The important thing is that they will soon question the idea of an "ad budget".

"Advertising won't work in my business"
Sometimes this prospect is beyond help. But here's what I say;
"You mean nobody in your business makes money from their advertising? *Nobody*?"
What you are trying to get them to say is "Well, I guess some people make it work, but it's never worked for me"
Then say "You must have had a bad experience advertising. *Could you tell me about it?*" (Or just "tell me about it")

You just want the prospect to spew out any prejudices against advertising. You want them to tell you what they did, and who they are mad at. It's very effective in easing their pain, and building rapport. Again, I've used it extensively, it always helps move the sale forward... if you'll let it.

"I've read that only 2% of all ads more than pay for themselves. Would you say that your ad may have been in the 98% that don't work?"
You don't need to use this question in any sequence. It just lets them know that their experience was not unusual. You might add "Would you like to know what the 2% that are consistently successful do?"

After they say "YES" to that little gem, just ask "Do you have a minute right now?"

And now you *better* know the answer to that question.

"Advertising won't work in my *area*"
This is very similar to the "Advertising won't work in my business" objection. The answers are the same, but the first question might be "You mean it doesn't work for *anyone* in your area?"

"I tried advertising before (or your company) and it didn't work" or "The last guy from your company was a jerk!"
You say "Oh? What happened?"
You just want them to have a chance to *vent*. After you hear their tale of woe, you are actually in a good position to ask qualifying questions and move the sale forward.

Say "I understand, and I don't blame you at all for your bad first impression of our company. The rep before should have known more about how to make your ads pay off, and he obviously didn't explain that most advertisers don't hit a home run the first time at bat. It was a stupid mistake on our part. What did the ad look like (sound like)?"

What the prospect will usually do is backtrack, and

tell you that you aren't to blame. Amazingly, this makes you look better in the customer's eyes than if he never advertised with you at all.

This is a pretty advanced concept. But I'll slip it in here (for the people reading the *whole* book) I'd rather talk to a prospect that is angry with our company, than a stranger. Why? Because the one who is angry is *emotionally involved.* And as soon as he sees that you are on his side, the scale tips rapidly in your favor. You may have to listen to unreasonable whining for twenty minutes or so, but the reward is there. Just don't act subservient. You are listening like a "concerned friend".... that's the key. And frankly, sometimes the client's complaint is legitimate.

If they tell you that the last guy was a jerk (I borrowed this from Tom Hopkins, and it's a gem) I ask "If you were our company, and found out that one of your reps was treating your clients badly... what would *you* do?" The answer is always "I'd fire them". Then you say "Well, that's what they did. We don't want to make the same mistakes twice. Do you mind if I ask you a few questions?" It's one of the few techniques I've read in a sales book that actually works as advertised. (Except for *this* book, of course!)

"I only advertise in the Yellow Pages/Radio/TV/Newspaper"

This is unreasoning. You hear this from people that advertise out of habit. They aren't tracking results. They aren't testing different media.

Here is an answer that will really work, most of the time.

"Yellow Pages is a good choice, and I appreciate that you are loyal to them. Tell me, How did you pick Yellow Pages, and what results do you see?"

At this point, you just want them to tell you about their advertising, and what notions they have about what good advertising is. Then you go on..

"I think you should stay with the Yellow Pages. It obviously works for you. And it attracts a certain percentage of your market. About 25% of the people go to the Yellow Pages when they are looking to purchase something. Now, what do you think you should do to let *the other 75%* know about what you have to offer?"

Let that sink in for a minute....

"What kind of calls do you get from the Yellow Pages? Is it mostly people looking to buy your high end product? Is it people asking for a price? Are they asking for service?" (The questions depend on the prospect's business.)

What you want the prospect to realize is that Yellow Page ads are attracting the price shopper mostly. And the average Yellow Pages caller calls 5.3 places, asking for prices, before they decide where to shop. (That statistic is from the actual Yellow Pages). Does your prospect want the lowest price shopper? Does he always have the lowest price? (I sure never did).

You can even add "The good news about Yellow Pages is; Everyone knows what it is, and everyone knows your phone number is listed. It's easy to find you. But the Yellow Pages *is the only advertising media that always has all your competitors listed right beside you.* Can you think of a reason that this might hurt your response?"

Let them think... and let them talk. They will soon see that they are missing a huge chunk of profitable business.

No matter what their "exclusive media" is, just compliment them on picking it, tell them what's good about it, and ask questions that lead them to discover that they are missing most of the available advertising profits out there.

"We promote our store on the internet"
This is slightly different from "We advertising in the Yellow Pages". Every smart businessperson

promotes their business online. It's cheap, the listings in search engines are free, and a website requires very little maintenance to stay profitable. Competing with the idea of advertising online will be a losing proposition. So don't compete.

First ask "Advertising online sounds like a smart idea. So you have a website? What kind of results are you getting?"
You just want the prospect to either brag about how sophisticated they are for advertising online, or complain because it isn't producing many sales. As I've said before, most clients don't track their ad results anyway, so he may not have any idea how well it works.

"One of the great things about having a good website to promote your business, is that you can get such a great result when people *see* it. And one of the greatest hidden benefits of advertising with us is letting people know you *have* a website, and directing prospects to the website so it can be even more effective. We always recommend that you put your website in every ad, that way you are talking to local shoppers who *don't* go online, as well as shoppers that *do*. It's not really a matter of advertising online *or* advertising in print/radio...... online marketing supports your print marketing, and your print marketing directs prospects to your website. They are the two halves of a solid profitable marketing plan. Does that make sense?"

"Your Competition Is Cheaper"
Sometimes that is legitimate. If the other media is identical to yours in every way; circulation, method of delivery, size, type of paper (in print), demographic of audience, frequency of delivery, and expertise in helping you craft a winning ad. But these things are rarely the same.
Let's say the media is the same. That's really the only time you'll get this. "Radio is cheaper than print" is silly, because they are completely different and have a completely different audience.

Say "And how are we the same as them to make the price comparison accurate?"

The prospect may actually talk himself out of this one. His information may be completely wrong. I have heard (after a short list of comparisons) a prospect say "Wait a minute. You go to 50,000 homes? Oh, well the other guys only go to 15,000 homes. Never mind".

Here's what works. You need to get the prospect away from the "Us *VS* Them" mentality... or the "Either Us *Or* Them" mentality.

"So your real concern is making sure that your ads are profitable, and you don't want to spend money on ads foolishly, is that right? Wouldn't you agree that the ad that generates the highest net profit is the cheaper ad?"

(Let that sink in, and explain what that means, if necessary)

"Here's what I suggest. Run an ad with them.. run one with us. Same size ad. Track the results, and I'll show you how. After even one ad, you'll see a clear winner. But you know what may happen? *Both* may produce a good profit. If that happens you'd be silly to stop using either one, isn't that right?"

Then you help them with *your* ad. If they use your suggestions in the other ad, so what?
(I wouldn't mention that to them, but don't complain if they do). Is your offer better than the other one? If it really is, this little experiment will bear that out. Hint; It helps if your ad comes out just a little ahead of the competitor's ad. If everything is *exactly equal* (Never happens), you'll get a tiny bump in response. If the public sees two identical offers a few days apart, the first ad will generate a few more people. Why? Because people don't come in twice on the same offer.

"I rely on word-of mouth for my business"
He does *now*. "Did you ever do advertising? Tell me about it."
After he winds down...
"You are absolutely right about word-of-mouth being the best advertising. It's better than what I have to offer, in fact. But profitable word-of-mouth comes from satisfied customers. So first, they have to *become customers* and *then* the word-of-mouth can come from *them*. Your advertising that you did in the past was what *created* a customer base in the first place, so that word-of-mouth could take hold. And those ads are still paying off today. Your word-of-mouth customers are proof of that. Would you like another surge in business, at no net cost, so you can get even more word-of-mouth in the future?"

OK (I know you're wondering), what's this "No net cost" business?

Well.....
If the client truly has a good word-of-mouth stream of customers, that means he's doing a lot right. He has a good reputation, and people spread the word about him. That makes advertising far more profitable for the client. It's far easier to make an ad pay when the people reading the ad already like and trust the client. You can even tell that to the client,

if you like. It will make your argument stronger.

And.... if the ad creates more net profit than it costs... the new customers it generated ..are ...*Free*.

"The big box stores are taking all my business. How can I compete?"

Ok, I cheated. This isn't really an objection to buying from you, but a complaint about business in general. Although the prospect may think it applies to buying advertising. Here's the silver bullet. "You're absolutely right. The big box stores *are* taking your business. And frankly, it's a losing proposition to try to compete with them on price. I wouldn't do it. But how many people buy *only* because of price? When you go to Wal-Mart, do you see *everyone* there? Of course not. You see "lowest price only" shoppers. And depending on the economy, that amounts to between 25-30% of the population. The rest of the population buy because of quality, service, knowledgeable staff, and selection. Of course, price is always important. Why would you even *want* to compete for the lowest 30% of the buyers... the *least profitable* 30%? It's far more profitable to cater to the middle and higher end buyer. And there are so many *more* of them!"

"We can't afford any advertising. The economy is killing us!"

At the time I'm writing this, we are in a major recession. Businesses really *are* hurting.
So you will hear variations of "We need to cut back on our advertising".

You are so fortunate that you sell a product that generates profit.... when the client needs it the most. In bad times, you cut back expenses... *not profit producing assets.*

"The economy is affecting most businesses. Are sales down?" They say "Yes", of course.
"So right now, the most important thing is to get as many buyers in here as possible, right?"
A smart merchant may say "I know where you're going with this".
Then you say "You should *absolutely* cut back on advertising... if the advertising isn't generating a profit. But what you need is not less advertising, but more *effective* advertising... advertising that generates a *profit*, is that right?". The client pretty much has to agree with that, or he's insane. Then you just say "Why don't I ask you a few questions to see if we can eliminate the bad ads, and stick with the good ones, OK?".

You should also know (and explain to the client)

that lessening your advertising doesn't create *more* business. It creates less business. And *hiding what you offer* (by not advertising) creates a self fulfilling spiral into less advertising... less business.... less advertising... less business.

As a business owner, and talking to thousands of business owners, I can tell you; The two absolute signs that a business is closing soon are 1) shorter Open hours... and 2) less advertising.
Together they will kill your business. Profitable advertising *feeds* your business. How else will the new customers know where to *buy*?

"Trying to save money by not advertising is like an employee trying to save gas money by not showing up for work." - Me

"My customers only buy the lowest price"
This is very much related to the above ("big box stores").
You say "May I see one of your ads? Maybe I can help".
Here's why this guy's customers only buy the cheapest stuff... because *that's who he's attracting with his ads*. That's the reason. If you are advertising on price alone, and stressing your low prices, you are attracting about 25% of the population... the diehard price-only shopper. And

you are ignoring the customers that buy because of service, quality, durability, ease of use, brand identity, and the fact that you are an expert there to answer their questions.

"If you advertise based on price only.... your business can be completely destroyed by anyone doing the simple act of charging less than you."
- Claude

"I wouldn't know what to advertise"
Here's where most reps make a mistake. They think that an ad with a picture of the owner, his dog, a picture of his store, the name of the business at the top, and a catchy slogan... are all this client needs to place an ad. That's just wrong.

Ask him "What do you sell a lot of?"
You want to advertise something that is popular *anyway*, not the inventory that nobody will buy at any price. "What do you make your most profit on?" Stay away from low priced loss leaders. If you advertise the lowest margin stuff, even a successful ad will lose him money.

"What are some of the advantages this product has over other products?" and "What advantages does the customer get from buying from you, instead of a competitor?" are two great questions that will lead to....... what to advertise, and what bullet points to put in the ad.

Have you seen McDonald's ads? Twenty five years ago, they advertised the cheapest things (hamburger, Coke, fries). Now they advertise *bundles* of food. They are called "Happy Meals", and at the register you could even Super-Size the meals. They have found that the people will buy the more expensive items (or bundles) if you just advertise them.

"I Just Want A Better Deal"......

Just say "When *you* are showing your customer exactly want they need... *at a fair price*... and *they* say 'I want a better deal'.. what do you say to *them*". This actually works most of the time. It's like the prospect is answering his own objection... from his point-of-view. Don't skimp on this one. Every word here has a purpose. I can't count how many times I've used this effectively.

"Do you guarantee that my ads will be profitable?"

This is more of a challenge to get rid of you than an actual question.

If you say "Yes", you're in trouble. If you say "No", then that's the end of the conversation.

I get this question (almost word for word) in my seminars. The answer I give is effective in a great percentage of cases.

"Of course not. It would be irresponsible of me to guarantee what someone *else* is going to do. But I can guarantee what happens if you *don't* advertise... Nothing. And if the ad takes a few tries before we get a message to market match.. then we'll keep working with you. Your success is our success. Fair enough?"

After you answer their questions and give all the information they need... I ask "May I make a recommendation?"

They always say "Yes". And then I show them the recommended solution/schedule/package/etc.

"I want to think about it"

I saved this one for last, because it's the only objection you will still get at the end of the presentation.... that you won't get at the beginning of the sales process. In fact, you'll usually get this objection *after* your closing question.

This may sound like I'm contradicting what I've said before, but bear with me.

Earlier I said that everyone buys at their own pace. That's certainly true. But there is a difference between gathering information to make a decision... and not being able to make a decision at all... ever. Some people just *stall*.

If you have been selling for any time at all, you know that you get "Yes"... "No"... or "Maybe" at the end of the sales process. "Yes" is great. "No" is completely acceptable to me.

But "Maybe"?

Lifetimes have been wasted trying to convert the "Maybe"s into sales. After you have established rapport... after you have answered every question the prospect has... after you have shown how advertising with you generates a profit... they may say "I just have to think about it".

They are not saying "Now's not a good time" or "I need to check with my partner". No, they are just allergic to saying "No".

Don't do this! I had a rep working for me selling in

people's homes. She was smart, talented, and a good closer. She called me at the office at the end of the presentation to see if I could help her. The prospect said "I just need to think about it". She raised her voice a little and said "I've been here for *three hours*... think *faster*!"

I couldn't help but laugh out loud. The prospect bought. I tried the same tactic about a dozen times, thinking it must be a great technique. Nope, it only worked for her... that one time.

This next technique usually gets them off the fence. You have probably heard of the "Alternate of choice close".

You could say "We have two different (schedules/down payments/sizes/frequencies/start dates/etc.) Which one sounds better to you *to get you started*?" If they can't decide, always recommend the less expensive or less imposing offer. Make it easier for them.

I learned this next idea from a master salesman that actually answered any stalling objection and nicely positioned me as the nice guy. I've used it extensively, and it works.

They say "I just need to think about it".

You say "I understand. Bob, my goal here was to make this offer so specific to your situation, so *obviously to your benefit* that you would say "yes" without hesitation. If I haven't done that, then you should just say "No". I only want clients that are absolutely looking forward to doing business with me. Is that you?"

Say it in a matter of fact way. Don't sound angry, condescending, or irritated. You are just one professional advisor giving advice.

You can't believe the number of times the client has then said to me "No, I'm sold. Let's do it."

If they say "No" to that, you're done. But at least you won't be wasting any more time *hoping* something happens.

And now we are ready for ....the *Close*.

"Advertising says to people, 'Here's what we've got. Here's what it will do for you. Here's how to get it."

-Leo Burnett

The Master Level Closing Technique

You just flipped to this chapter *first*, didn't you?

What I'm going to tell you about closing is different from what you have read in a book, or maybe been taught. But I promise you, what you are about to be learn is told after over 10,000 in-home presentations, after countless hours analyzing what worked and what didn't, and after attaining a very high closing rate.

Many salespeople watch a master salesperson in action and think that it was their *close* that got the sale. As if there is a Magic Phrase that you can say that instantly turns a buyer from "Not interested in buying" to "Signing on the dotted line". It doesn't exist.

First, let me say that your client may not be ready to buy. Maybe they have a question unanswered. Maybe they just need time for the whole process to "sink in". Usually the whole process can happen in one visit, but not always. After selling (and paying attention) for a few years, you'll gain a sense of when they are at the end of gathering information. *Then* I make the recommendation. And *then* I deliver the close. It isn't magic. You can't just jump up in the middle of a conversation and say "Well? Are you ready or not?".

Ready?
I show them my solution (usually on a form of some sort) or just tell them what it is, and say;

"Is that OK?" or "Is that right?" After they say "yes", just write it up.

Now close that mouth that's hanging open.

Here's how master salespeople sell; Every anticipated objection is answered *in the presentation*. If the objection comes up in the qualifying questions, you answer it *before* the presentation.

The presentation is *planned and built* around any possible reason for saying "No". If you are working *with* the prospect (as opposed to just talking *at* them), they know that your recommendation is for *their* benefit, as well as yours.

If you skipped to this chapter, you really need to go back and read the rest of the book. I promise... this will make sense.

Picture this; The client says "I want this, and this, and this, and this, and this!"
You say "Ok, I'll give it to you"
The client can't possibly say "No".. It's simply anti-human.

Now, that was an extreme oversimplification of the sales process, I know. But essentially, you are explaining how advertising absolutely benefits the client.. *until the client understands and believes it*. You are showing them a painless way to pay for the advertising (out of the profits that advertising earns), and you are showing them how to do it in the most profitable way. You are then answering all their questions *to their satisfaction.*

When I'm selling, the sale either breaks down very quickly (there is something keeping us from moving forward) or they say "Yes". Not every time, but often enough for me to *expect* it.

Selling is a process between you and the client. It isn't a *challenge*. They want more profit, you want them to *make* more profit. Where's the argument?

When you get prospects saying "No" to you, you just didn't answer their questions to their satisfaction, or you didn't solve a problem that kept them from buying. Your idea didn't get *through*....

But that's all OK. Maybe you didn't finish the sales process. That's why you go back. Many times you can't finish the sale in one call, maybe most times. The client simply hasn't gone through everything they need to go through before they are ready... and you didn't recognize that.

Am I making it sound like it's your responsibility to sell. Am I making it sound like it's your fault that they don't buy? That's because it is.

A Master Salesman once told me "About 20% of the people you see are closed minded, ignorant people who simply won't buy anything from anyone. You can't reach them no matter what you do. About 20% of the people you see will buy anything. You can't talk them out of it. They just love to buy. The other 60% is entirely up to you". Your exact percentages may vary a tad, but it's a good estimate of what is out there.

When I sold in home, the first several years.... I would give my canned presentation first, deferring any questions until the end. Then I would spend an hour (or two or three) *closing*.
It wore them out and wore me out too.

That's a stupid way to make a living.

Eventually I figured out that, if I just asked them plenty of qualifying questions up front, and then tailored my presentation to answer any objections that they brought up (or that I thought they *would* bring up), and made the offer custom fit their *exact* situation.... my closing percentage skyrocketed. Why? Because I was concentrating on what *they* wanted. And then I showed them how my product would *exactly fit* into what they wanted. It's very hard to say "No" to *that*.

Personally, I would write out that last paragraph, post it on the wall, and read it every day. I just gave you *the secret*.

Friend, I've read more books on closing that anyone I know. I've said closes that were perfectly rehearsed, perfectly executed. And worked ...occasionally. But that was OK, because I was *still closing*. I had memorized so many closes that I could close for four hours, and never repeat myself. Here's the problem.... the customer didn't want to *buy*. So selling became a contest of wills. Selling isn't a contest, it's a service. It's a contest when you are thinking of what *you* want. It's a service when you think about what the *client* wants. It's that simple.

A Few Closes That Actually Work.
These little goodies actually will tip a buyer over the edge, if they are thinking about buying *anyway*. They just give the client an extra reason to buy.

Scarcity; When you are calling clients... If you only have one page left... that's not the time to drop the price by saying "I'll give you my last page for half price". No, No, No. Now's the time to call and say "I just found out that we have *only one page left*. I'm calling you because I didn't want you to miss out."

If this is true, use; "I only have one page left. This book filled up so quick this month. Do you want me to call just to make sure that last page wasn't taken?" I actually used almost the exact same close once with a CEO. He said "That's a heck of a close". I said "Thanks, did it work?". We both laughed, and of course he bought... just like he was going to anyway. It just made the process a little faster.

When closing say "This is what I *recommend*" and then just list quickly the points of the agreement. It's a psychological point that if they reject your idea... and you *recommended* it... they are rejecting you as a person. They aren't really, but they will feel that way. This really only works if trust has been established, and there is a rapport between you.

This also works extremely well if they are considering two options. And you better pick the one that is *better* for them... and not the one that pays you more (unless that really is the better option) "I recommend this one" is strong. But you better have a darn good reason.... because they may ask "OK, *why* is this one better for me?". So only use it when you are *sure*.

Recommend something *less* than what they were thinking.

Not by much, but I'll say "May I recommend that you not take the 'full color' option. Everyone else on that page will be in full color. Black & white will be less expensive... and will actually make your ad

stand out from the others. What do *you* think?"
I say that even before they said they were interested in full color. Of course, you adapt this to your offer. It sets me up to recommend bigger things later... like *that they buy* ...from *me* ...right *now*.

Lots of *small easy decisions* instead of one big one;
I hesitate telling you about this, because if it sounds like a technique it may backfire. But if they have to make a final minor choice, sometimes it will carry the sale. For example; "Should we put the headline in quotations?". It's a minor point, and easy decision. And if you sprinkle your recommended schedule/print order with these minor choices, it will pretty much carry the sale. Don't use this until you are in the "Let's figure out the order for you" stage. I use this method so much in my presentations, it's done unconsciously. And it works so well that it's one of the reasons people watching me sell thought I must have used some magic close.

The main difference between a 20% closer... and an 80% closer.
I'm assuming that, for this example, everything has been done the same up until you ask them to buy. Here's where most people lose the sale.;
They act *nervous* when they get near the close. They may sweat a little, their voice way waver, they

may hesitate at the close. These are all signals to the prospect that... *you are not comfortable asking them to buy*. You can tell when a rep doesn't *expect* to make the sale. You can also tell when the rep absolutely expects you to buy.... not in an arrogant way, but in a confident matter-of-fact way.

Amazingly, prospects *expect* you to ask them to buy. And when you hesitate, stammer, mumble, fidget, or beat around the bush at the close... the prospect thinks *something is wrong*.

Perhaps the biggest reason that my closing percentage is higher than average, next to qualifying with questions, is that I act like the last hundred people said "Yes" to me. Prospects get the strong impression that "Buying from Claude" is the most natural, and expected, thing to do.
This takes practice. Roll play with another rep. If possible, find a great... *Great* sales rep.. it doesn't matter what he sells... and ask if you can ride with them for the day. See how they handle themselves.

I had one rep call me to ask if I could ride with him to see what he was doing wrong. This was again when I was selling in people's homes.

His product presentation was flawless... far better than mine. He had rapport from the beginning. He built value in what he sold, and the people were excited to see what he was selling. Then the time came for him to ask them to buy. He refused.

He would change the subject, start talking about their house, or kids, or whatever. I watched as their *desire to buy* slowly leaked out of the room.

After an hour of this agony, I finally said "Would you guys like to buy one?".
The wife said "Oh, are these for sale? Sure we want one!".

I've seen similar travesties with other reps. Some people freeze at the thought of asking the prospect to buy. But if you *don't ask prospects to buy*, and they don't buy?

You have *wasted their time*.

When I had sales reps working for me, I would have them call from the customer's home to give us credit information... and so I could help them close.

The rep calls me and says "I got a sale. They are writing out a check right now. Man, I needed this sale... I haven't had a sale in a month!"

Claude the Merciless; "Can they hear you?"

Unaware terrible rep; "Sure".
Claude: "You just killed your sale. Before you leave, they will come up with a reason why they can't buy. Even if they have already written the check. Call me back after you leave"

Of course, they told him that they forgot about something that made it *impossible* for them to buy right now. And he left empty handed. The rep made it clear, by his one statement, that buying from him was *unnatural*.... that it was the *wrong thing to do*. Most reps do this, and they never know.

Customers are looking for a feeling of certainty when they are buying. They are looking for assurance that this is the natural thing to do, and that everyone you see wants what you have. They have to get those feelings from *you*, After all, *you're the only other person in the room..*

You should have two attitudes when selling;

> 1) You are there to help the prospect make more money... not so you can make more money.
> 2) The most natural and expected thing for them to do is take your recommendation and buy from you.

If you genuinely have those attitudes when you talk

to a prospect, your sales will multiply, I promise.

Don't take it personally, either way.
You'll get advice like "Don't take rejection personally". Good advice whether you are prospecting, presenting, or closing. But you also can't take *getting the sale* personally either.

When you are new, you'll get a rush from every sale. You'll be in the dumps every time a prospect says "No".
But think about a surgeon. Does he do a dance every time a patient survives surgery and gets better? No. It's all *expected*. It's *normal* that everything goes well. And the surgeon conveys that in every patient contact, from the first office visit to recovery.

You may have gone ten appointments without one single sale, but the next customer you see can never know that.

"Wow. You're A Great Salesperson"
If they say that after they buy... it's a compliment. If they say it before they buy... it's a trap.
The client is attributing your sales skills as the reason they want to buy. This is a mental game they play to justify why they aren't buying. It isn't usually a real compliment (unless they have already bought).

I have found that this works; "I appreciate that, but really I'm not a great salesperson, it's just that this is such a great idea *for you*... don't you think so?"

See? ...you are not great ...your *advertising offer* is great.

"The very best advertising is Word Of Mouth from satisfied customers. But you first need to advertise to get those customers."

-Claude Whitacre

Visit with ideas

Visit with ideas, and then they will need to advertise to get the idea out.

This works even with existing clients. If you give the client a reason (to their benefit) to advertise beyond what they are doing now, you can make an additional sale. This works with new clients too.

Here are a few ideas;
Event advertising; Is it a holiday? Someone's Birthday? Was there just a huge sports game that the local town won? Did the business just open, expand, move? Is the owner going on vacation?

Did the new models (of whatever) just come out?

These are all reasons to advertise *now*.

These are all events. But events tend to repeat... and the events change very quickly. Surely you can think of one event happening each month. Ask the client to help. These are all reasons to advertise, and they have a huge built-in advantage. They all have a *deadline* that will make sense to the consumer.

Cause advertising; To be fair, this isn't a method I've used in my retail business. I learned about this very late in the game. It is a method I've used in my speaking business. Retail trainer Bob Negen covers this subject in great depth in his book **Marketing Your Retail Business**. I highly recommend it. I have retail clients who have used this method, so I know it works.

Essentially, you offer any local "Cause" (It can be a charity, church, or worthwhile group) a donation of a certain percentage (20% is common) for any business it's members give you. Or you can have the Cause mail out your Special Offer to it's mailing list. "20% of any purchase when you bring in this letter will be donated to the local animal shelter" is a powerful enticement to a list of donors to the shelter. The one thing I will tell you is, remember that this is a marketing idea. It *will* help any Cause you get to participate, and you can do this with several Causes at the same time. So you want to remember that *you are not making money off a charity*. They are making money because of your sales. Unless it's a charity (or any Cause) that you genuinely want to get involved with... keep it a business relationship.

Recruitment advertising; Your clients hire from time to time. Some hire continuously. Why not advertise for that perfect employee with *you*? I have even seen a full page newspaper ad... for a wife! (And Yes, he found one from the ad)

$5 Gift Certificate (or $10 or $20)
This is a brilliant idea I learned from my fellow retailer Howard Anderson. It works so well that I can say with confidence... it's going to work with any client.

Just make the ad a Gift Certificate for a certain dollar amount. You can make it for *new customers only*... although I wouldn't. And don't put a "$5 Gift Certificate good on any purchase over $50" either. That's a coupon... not a Gift Certificate. I've used this idea extensively with great results. Will some people just bring in a $10 Gift Certificate, buy something for $10 and walk out the door? Sure, maybe even most. But if you track the results (It's easy to track Gift Certificate sales. Just write the amount of the sale on the back of the Gift Certificate), you'll always make a profit. In my case, about one out of five people buy a high end product... but the Gift Certificate brought them in. We net about $8 for every $1 in Gift Certificates redeemed.

And remember, $10 in merchandise doesn't cost $10, It may cost $5.

10% off won't make it.

The offer in the ad must be good enough to create demand. It's better to give something for free with purchase, than to discount price. The customers like it more, and it costs the retailer less. A $10 Gift Certificate will dramatically out-pull a "10% off" offer. Even when "10% off" is more than $10.

Do you discount your ads to get that first ad from a new client?

Don't lower your price on the first ad. There are several things you can do that still maintain your price integrity.

You can barter for a portion of the first ad. But don't ever do it for the second ad... or that's the only way the customer will buy... because now they are trained (by *you*) to buy that way.

You can use a Gift Certificate on the first ad. Of course, this is really just a discount... but clients won't see it that way.

Give a free ad...*if* they buy a full page (right now, because the half page is available) they get an additional half page ad for free.
Of course, all these ideas are more profitable if you are selling a contract instead of a one shot ad.

If you just give a discount on your first ad... guess what? That discounted price just becomes.. *the price*.

And it will be near impossible to raise the price later.

"If your advertising goes unnoticed, everything else is academic."

-William Bernbach

In A Sales Slump? *Here's* The Way Out

I've done a study of Sales Slumps. I've hired, trained, and worked with hundreds of reps (in many fields), and I've kept thorough records. And I can tell you with absolute certainly. If you are in an extended slump... you simply aren't prospecting.

"But Claude, I put in twelve hour days!". No you don't. I *used* to think I did too. For over two decades, I kept meticulous records of how many prospecting calls I made, how many calls my reps made, how many presentations, and how many sales.

When I was in a slump (sure, it happens to everyone) I would sharpen my pencil, keep accurate records of what I did during the day, and I didn't *lie*.
I would always find that I simply wasn't working as much. I would create activity that *felt* like work.... but I wasn't really working.

A typical conversation with one of my reps (that worked for me) would be;
Him; "Claude, This business stinks. Nobody is buying, I can't make any money."
Claude the Merciless: "Let's look at the weekly activity. I see last week you only made two presentations and only prospected for two hours. The total time last week that you worked was six hours, plus or minus an hour. You made one sale, and made $500. Six hours of effort gave you $500. It's a great business. Let's see if we can make you *busier*, OK?"

Trust me, that's *not* what they wanted to hear.

It's a spiral. You have a bad day or two... you stop feeling "up"... so you avoid what makes you feel bad (being rejected by prospects, maybe)... which means you work less... which means you get worse results... which means you work even less...

See?

Here's the cure. I call it my "One Pushup Cure". Have you ever done a pushup? Can you do 100 pushups? (Neither can I)

Think of prospecting as doing 100 pushups. You won't even get started if it's that big of a job.

So what do I do? I decide that "today I'm only going to do one pushup".

But even when you only do one pushup, you still have to get ready. You have to get into position. And then I do one pushup. And guess what? I feel like a fool for only doing one. After all, it was pretty effortless. It didn't hurt, and I'm already down on the floor in position. So I'll do as many as I can.

But I convinced myself that I was only going to do one pushup.

I am going to confess something. I cold called for a couple of decades. I was great at it... but I hated doing it. I never enjoyed a single part of it. I'm not a social person by nature, and I don't enjoy meeting strangers. I have to force myself to do it. Everything else about selling is attractive to me, but not cold calling. So what did I do? (And still do today)?

I used to tell myself "after I knock on one door, I can quit". Of course, I still had to get dressed, get in the car, drive to where I was going to work, and walk up to the first door. And then I knocked.

And of course, nothing bad happened. Nobody yelled at me. And... I was already out there...

"I'd have to be a damn fool not to knock on at least one more door" I would tell myself. And after a few more tries, I was in a groove, and didn't mind so much.

One pushup... one door... one phone call.

Now I call people on the phone. "One call. That's it, and then I can get back to writing that book". Then I get my list of trade associations (or whoever I'm calling) and make the next call... and the next..... and in four hours of talking to new people I've had an extremely profitable day.

"But I'm only going to make that one... quick... call." Claude's One Pushup Cure.

The Reality Of Goal Setting... And How To Really Reach Your Goals

Goal setting is fun. "I'm going to be a millionaire in ten years" sounds great... and I'm not trying to talk you out of it (or any goal... Really).

But what happens after you set your five, ten, or twenty year goals? Most of us go back to what we were doing. After all, what we do today will have little impact on what we accomplish in twenty years... right? Maybe.

I always kept (and keep) my goals by the month. Sure, I know what I want in a year, but I want a deadline that's in the near future.

When I was selling in people's home.... I had income goals. For several years (in the 1970's and 80's) that was usually $1,000 a week. Later, that rose to $2,000 a week. That was more than a goal, it was *my schedule*.

So I did whatever it took to make that amount by the week. I didn't get paid by the week, I got paid by the sale... but I counted by the week. Saturday was the day I started for the following week.

And here is how I guaranteed that I met my goal; I made sure I was ahead of my weekly goal. I didn't wait until Friday... and then panic. Saturday was a busy day. I usually made half of my week's goal on Saturday. Then I worked until I made my goal. Then I worked so I had a head-start on the next week's schedule. On rare occasions, I would be behind at the end of the week .I carried over the negative to the next week. I never had a negative two weeks in a row. I did that for over twenty years. Did I want to take a week off to travel, vacation, go to a convention, speak? Then I factored that in, and made sure I was far enough ahead in my earnings that I wouldn't get behind.

But here's what made it work; I re-tallied all my figures after each sale. I knew after each call where I was for the week. I looked at my sales and commission totals at least daily.

I wanted to *know* where I stood. And if you want your financial goals to work for you.. you'll break them down to weekly, then daily goals.... and you make them your *schedule*.

If you don't do this, your goals become fantasies.

"The great lie in every argument is that one side is actually correct"

-Claude Whitacre

Collecting The Money

Whatever your company's schedule is in customer payment, don't let it slip away from you. If your customer isn't paying you on time, it's because that's how you have *trained* him to pay.

Believe me, some of his suppliers don't tolerate late payments... and he pays *them* on time.

Merchants who actually pay you... but pay late, are doing it out of habit. The difference between a person who drives a car with the gas tank hovering on empty and the person who always has a full tank... is *one* tank of gas over their entire lifetime. It's a habit.

One tip; It's a lot better to get a post-dated check that have them promise to mail it in by the same date. In his mind, a post-dated check means he's already paid you. He may have to put *another* supplier off for a few weeks, because he wrote you that check, and the date (he wrote on the check) arrived.

Also; Let them make partial payments. If they don't have the whole amount, take half, or a third. It's a whole lot easier to collect the second half of a bill, than the entire thing. Try to get a post dated check for the second half.

I also might add... if the client's ads are profitable.. and he *knows* it. You are in a far stronger position to collect.

Selling Advertising With Seminars

How to use seminars to *explode* your business.

Your BIG problem; After you sell the space, the advertiser doesn't have a clue as to how to make the ad profitable.... But they *think* they do. So they will take any recommendations from you with a grain of salt. Their thought is "I know my business better than this ad rep". After all, they don't know you well..... yet.

So they do what everyone does. They put a picture of their puppy in the ad... put the name of their business at the top of the ad (in huge letters)... and come up with a cute statement about "we service all makes & models". Ta Da! Brilliant.

Then the ad runs... nothing happens.. and to the advertiser "This ad media doesn't work"... *and they will never use it again*. They are *lost*. And to the advertiser, *it's your fault*.

One problem is that they think they are in the "mattress, furniture, bicycle, flower, or home improvement business" (or whatever field they are in). They *do* know more about *what* they sell than you. You can't teach them more about what they sell, and that's not what they need from you. They need to know more about "Getting people to come in to buy". They need to think of themselves as being in the "Marketing of their product" business. The difference is huge.

But human nature being what it is, you can't easily convince them to see advertising differently... and you can't do it in an hour. They need to hear it from an independent, unbiased, respected, authority figure. You can hire that person, find them in your ranks, or contract the job out. There are books on small business advertising that you can give as gifts to your prospects, but some people won't read them.

My retail store sells high end vacuum cleaners. I'm in the "Marketing of vacuum cleaners" business. When you are in my store discussing advertising..... and you think of yourself in the "Selling of ad space" business... there will be a disconnect between the two of us.
When you are selling me advertising.... you need to be in the "Marketing of vacuum cleaners" business too. Why? Because I don't want to buy advertising... but I *do* want to sell more vacuum cleaners. And **Advertising is Selling**.

You need better, well informed, motivated clients.

Enter the advertising seminar
The purpose of having your prospects and clients attend an advertising seminar is to change their thinking about what advertising is. They need to realize that the money is in the *marketing* ...not the product they sell. When you and your client are both thinking "How can we sell more (of whatever they sell)", you become an asset to them, instead of "just another ad rep".

Advantages; They will learn how to advertise (biggest thing, but only in your media), and what to expect from advertising. Managing the client's expectations is a real key to making them happy. Teaching them the benefit of tracking ad results is a key to keeping them happy. Teaching them how to advertise profitably will make them feel smarter than their competition. And they will be.

You will be a consultant, not a pitchman.. They will be sold on your company, media, and you. Referrals will be better, because the client can brag to their buddies about their advertising results.

One thing you can't avoid in a person-to-person sales situation, is that the client is buying *in a bubble*. They have nobody else saying that "it's a good idea". Most people want to hear from other people that what they are considering is a good idea, that buying from you is *normal*, and that other people have tried it and like it. It's called Social Proof. In sales letters, testimonials provide the social proof. It's far more powerful when done in person. And nothing will create fast client acquisition like a well run seminar.

In any seminar, there is a "group mentality". If you already have a few attendees that have had good results, make sure you ask them to share their results. Unbiased results shared have far more power than anything you could say.

You want to create a Feeding Frenzy. Far easier to

do in a group than one-on-one.. At the end of the seminar, you should have most of the attendees eager.... chomping at the bit... to buy from you. Won't that be a pleasant change?

If you conduct advertising seminars, and gather referrals from your happy clients, you'll be busy seeing people *who can't wait until you show up*. So you want to do this right.
Another huge benefit to seminar selling is that it quickly fills out your media. If you sell direct mail in envelopes, it gives you a full envelope. If you sell newspaper advertising, it fills out the newspaper with more ads. A magazine format becomes thicker.

Why is this important?
When you show your sample (of your media) to your prospect, it offers *social proof* that your advertising works, and it works for businesses in varied categories. Advertisers like to see newspapers full of ads.

For example, have you ever driven into a parking lot of a restaurant... and the parking lot is empty? I have. We don't go in. An empty parking lot is practically screaming "Nobody eats here!". It's the same with advertising space (or time on the radio or TV).

Does your local newspaper have far less ads than it

did five years ago? The paper is getting thin. What does that tell the businesses in your town? "Nobody can make an ad work in this newspaper". Advertisers want to go where the action is.

And now a dose of reality;
Even when the seminar is free, it must be *sold*. If you invite 100 people to your seminar, don't just expect them to show up. First, you need them to register. This can be as simple as giving them an invitation, and having them tell you that they will be there. But here is a reality; most people won't show up. If 100 people *promise* that they will be there, prepare for about 30-35 to actually show. If it rains that evening it will be even less. That's one reason you give a gift for showing up, and they know about it. Some will show up just to get the gift. That's okay. This is also a reason that you need to hand them (or mail them) a sales letter explaining what they will gain from attending. And if you are inviting these people in person, you need to start at least two weeks before the seminar. Seeing 200-300 people, to get 100 to say they will show up, takes time.

You will also need to confirm that they are showing up the day before. Sometimes I've called the same day as the seminar. People forget. You'll double your attendance by verifying the day before (or the same day) that they will show up.

You need to keep a record of the people that said they were attending. You will need their E-Mail address, phone number and business name and address. Why? Because you'll need to verify that they are showing up. Verify by E-Mail and then by phone. That's right, do both. Many people won't get the E-Mail (or will get it too late), and it's harder to say "No" over the phone.

You'll also want to know who said they were going to show up because you can offer the same seminar multiple times. Even in a small city (under 25,000 population) you may find it productive to offer the seminar every month, until you begin to run out of businesses to invite. But you *always* invite the people who didn't show up before. And you *always* invite the previous attendees. They will help build excitement at the seminar, and provide proof that the information provided actually works.

A trap that many fall into when doing these seminars is thinking that the purpose of the seminar is to teach. It's not. Teaching will take place, but the purpose is to sell the client on advertising profitably.... with you, and doing it now (or at the appointment). So a dry "information dump" will fail.

Registration script; (this is what reps say when *I'm* doing the seminar).

Introduce yourself...

"Have you noticed a difference in your ad response in this economy? Maybe we can help. On Tuesday, April 7th, we are putting on a seminar at the Holiday inn at 6:30PM. It's a two hour seminar titled **How To Use Advertising To Survive And Thrive In Our Economy**. It will be put on by the author of the **Unfair Advantage Small Business Advertising Manual**. The seminar will cover all kinds of advertising, and the presenter will stay afterwards to answer any questions. Everyone who attends will also get the $39...8 CD course **Small Business Advantage** for *free*.. Refreshments will be made available. There is no charge for the gift or the seminar, and we won't be selling advertising there. I have set aside two tickets in your name. Would you like to come?"

Registering prospects for the seminar is prospecting.

I hear from ad reps occasionally "I don't have time to register prospects for this seminar. I need to spend my time prospecting for new business and selling". Inviting prospects to this seminar is *prospecting*. The seminar itself acts as a presentation to sell people on the idea of advertising... advertising with *you*... and advertising *now*. Then after the seminar, all the rep has to do is make the appointment, and work out the advertising schedule. The best results I've seen is when a team of advertising reps invests the entire two weeks before the seminar, *solely* in inviting prospects and registering them. Half hearted efforts produce zero results here. Each rep should be averaging seven to ten solid reservations a day for the two week period. Anyone can do that.

Registering by mail, in person, by phone, or by E-Mail

Everyone wants to send E-Mail. It's free, fast, and almost effortless. But you need the E-Mail address. And you may as well get that as you register them for the seminar. E-Mail is to remind them to show after they register. Don't use it as the primary method of getting registrations.

By phone; If your client base is far away... or if they are already established clients... using the phone will speed up the process. The script is about the same as in person. And you can hire out the phone work, if you like.

By mail; Postcards work. The problem is that you will need to mail out 5,000 postcards to get 30 people to register. Even at bulk rates, you looking at 30 cents each to mail. If you are only mailing to existing clients, a sales letter (explaining what will be in the seminar) followed up by a phone call will be productive.

In person; If you want to get the highest turnout, this is the way. It's especially productive if you don't know the people you are inviting. You'll be there to answer questions, build rapport, and establish that you would be their rep if they decide to advertise with you. You should also be at the seminar itself to greet them. Another reason to be at the seminar is that, right after the seminar, you'll want to set up an appointment with them to discuss advertising with you.

A recommended and fair policy is; The rep who invited them, gets them as a client after the seminar.

Registration And Activity Form

Attending?	Business Name	Attendee Name	Phone	E-Mail

You need a sheet that you can write the information on when you register someone for the seminar. The information on the last page is all you really need. I would even get the business name and name of everyone you *invite*. That acts as verification that the rep is actually inviting people to the seminar, and they will have a record if someone they invited (but says they can't *attend*) shows up anyway. The rep will still get that prospect as a client. This also lets you know if the attendee was invited *at all*. You should call the day of the seminar to tell them that you have reserved their table (or seat).

An idea I have seen that really stimulates registrations is a bonus for the most registrations that actually attend. That bonus is paid to the rep, and is typically $50 or $100.

A typical program is $50 to any rep that gets 20 attendees from the people he registers, and another $50 goes to the rep who has the most attendees from the people he registered.

Of course, all the reps get the profits from the ad sales generated. This bonus is in addition to that.

Advertise in your media: Of course, you advertise. You put an invitation in your advertising media. Your cost is low, and it will bring in a few more attendees. The trap is that some advertising reps will depend on the ad to bring people in, and will ignore inviting people in person. This will always fail.

Calendar of events: Almost every newspaper has a Calendar of Events. You can list your seminar there, and provide information about what will be taught there. Make sure you say that it's for business owners only, or you'll be swimming in people that just want to get a free meal, and see what's going on.

To feed or not to feed?

Many seminars feature a meal. These are usually in the evening. I prefer not to include a meal. Here's why; A meal offered *will* boost attendance, I promise. The problem is that you (or your presenter) will have to fight for the attendees attention while they are eating, and making the clanging noises that will be a constant at the seminar. Also, if you serve a meal, you will be fighting the small talk that always happens during meals. If you are talking to a very small group (maybe 40 or less) this will be manageable. But if you book the seminar in a hotel, you are also paying for a meal... even if they don't show up.

The exception is if you book the seminar in a restaurant. You must makes sure they have a banquet room. You will want to see it, before you commit to the booking. Cramped attendees aren't happy. Hot or cold attendees aren't happy. Is there plenty of lighting? Is there a musty smell? Will the room seat 50 people comfortably? You may have that many register.. or more.

The room must be completely closed off from the rest of the restaurant! A partition is not acceptable. Your room will be making noise, and the patrons in the restaurant will be making noise. Trust me, you want a separate room.

Of course, the main question is; Will the restaurant be willing to barter the event for advertising space. Almost nothing has a greater markup than rooms and food. Barter at full retail value on both sides. Have the owner attend the seminar. It's a Win-Win-Win.

If there is a meal, schedule it for 6:30 PM. That way you can start the seminar at 7:00PM.
By 7:00 most of the ordering and delivering of food will be over..... people will have settled on eating and drinking coffee or other beverage, and you can begin the seminar without too much noise. The half an hour is also used to meet people, get them seated, and have them get their food orders.

Don't serve alcohol... Don't serve alcohol... Don't

serve alcohol. People get louder, easier to anger, and listen less after a couple of drinks. Don't do it. No exceptions. The attendee that insists on a drink is the one that will ruin it for everyone after a couple drinks. Trust me. And make it clear to the restaurant owner that drinks won't be served. One way out is to simply book the seminar at a place that doesn't serve alcohol.

If more that 20 people show up, you'll need a microphone. Count on it. Make sure the restaurant or hotel has a sign in the lobby (or entrance) announcing your seminar... and giving the time and location in the facility. If people can't find the room fast, many will leave.

Make sure you reserve the room at least two weeks before the event. Three weeks is better. You need time to promote.

I would give a *great gift* for showing up. Usually I give a set of CDs on promoting your small business. It has a high perceived value, and fits in with my preferred attendee. If we don't offer a meal, we do offer beverages and sometimes cookies or pizza. Pizza is popular. It takes the place of a meal, but gets rid of most of the noise... and expense. We offer these light snacks because the seminar is in the evening... after work. And we don't want them thinking about their supper... and how hungry they are. Plus, soft drinks, coffee, and cookies will keep them awake. It may even convince everyone that it's the *speaker* that has them all excited! (That was a joke)

Best time of day? Best day of week? Best location?

I like evening seminars. Maybe starting at 6:30 or 7:00. We usually tell the people to be there at 6:30. The beverages are there and so is the pizza. The seminar starts at 7:00 sharp. If you tell them 6:30, it will allow for some late arrivals. Also, most people will be done eating before the seminar starts. The best days are Tuesday, Wednesday, and Thursday. Any day will work, but these are the days that most people have open. Make sure there is no huge local event or holiday on the day of the seminar. Believe me, if you are competing with trick-or-treat... you'll lose.

Daytime seminars are more attractive to employees. But evening seminars are more desirable for business owners.

I like hotel meeting rooms. A restaurant is okay as long as it's a meeting room. Make sure it's attractive and easy to find.

You can also book lunch time seminars.
The only problem is that you'll have less time to present. Most people take an hour for lunch, even the business owners. After they drive to the restaurant, you may have 45 minutes to present... including answering questions. If you can present your case that quickly, It's a valid way to do seminars. See if you can build a 20 minute speech that promotes the need for advertising information, and then invite them to your free seminar. It's always better to finish early, and answer questions... than to finish late.

You can also speak at the Rotary Club, Chamber of Commerce, and referral groups. In fact, anywhere business owners (not in the same business) gather. These opportunities can be used to promote the seminar or to give a mini-seminar. If your main seminar is only a week away, promote *that* seminar. If you don't have another seminar to promote, just give a few strong tips on advertising, show how your media may fit their business and ask for cards of anyone who wants to know more. Just don't eat the chicken.

Verification script the day of the seminar.
If you call the day of the seminar, you'll double the chance of them actually showing up.

You need to remind them that you have reserved their seat (or meal).... that you have set aside a gift for them.... and that you look forward to seeing them.

"Hi ____ this is ____. I'm just calling the attendees for this evening's meal and advertising seminar. Your seat is reserved, and your $39 gift is waiting for you to pick up. I just wanted to remind you that it starts at 6:30. Do you know how to get there? Were you planning on bringing a guest?"

The key here is to say... without pause... the first three sentences. The people need to feel like they are *obligated*. A reserved seat? A free gift? A free meal? They pretty much have to show up, don't they?

Don't be boring.
This takes a few forms. If your delivery is dry... if you are extremely nervous in front of groups... have someone else do it. It's hard to keep people interested for an hour in what you are saying. Also, don't just stand behind a podium and talk. Walk around, show examples of ads. Ask questions to get the audience involved.

The Content

An outline may be ;

- Ask the group questions to establish that they are getting something out of the seminar.

- Describe Return On Investment, and Tracking Ad Results.

- Compare forms of advertising

- Explain why your media works with the others.

- Give some information to improve ad results (You can use **The Unfair Advantage Small Business Advertising Manual** as a… well... manual)

- Concentrate on examples of ads using your media.

- Offer a special incentive to advertise with you... available to seminar attendees only.

USE GREAT BAIT!
Offering a seminar on advertising sounds great, but people need to show up. What do they get for showing up besides listening to you talk? I use CD programs on small business as a gift for attendance. We talked about serving a meal. That certainly helps.

A free drawing for a Gift Certificate is a smart idea. The Gift Certificate should be from a local merchant and be something that everyone would want. A certificate for free cigars won't work, but a $50 certificate at a nice local restaurant would do the trick. I would mention this when you register the people. You may even want to have a "free dinner for four" at the same restaurant that is hosting the seminar. Of course, you can barter ad space for the certificate. Announce the winner at the end of the seminar. Make it a drawing out of a hat or bowl.

Premiums to buy.
People who are attracted to a free meal are not the same people who are attracted to a free CD set on improving your business. The CD set (or book on marketing/advertising) will bring in the learners..... the people interested in improving their business... the people who want to *know more*.

That's why I prefer educational items as premiums

instead of a free umbrella. The free meal will increase attendance, but I also want the people eager to learn.

Don't just pitch.
If you spend the whole time telling everyone about your advertising company... and how great it is... you end up with a group of bored, testy, people who will vow to never go to another "free dinner" as long as they live. Your seminar must provide real value to the attendee... whether they buy later from you or not. You want to put on this seminar again and again... in the same area. Great word of mouth by past attendees will make each seminar easier to fill, and more fun to give.

Invite happy clients, they will help sell for you.
Absolutely a must. If you already have happy clients, invite them too. They will help support any claims you give. They will give you case examples (called testimonials) to show at the seminars, and they will make the room feel more friendly to you, and the other attendees. If you joke with them a little, and call them alumni.... they will make the new people more prone to buy. They will want to "Join the club".

Have a great reason for them to buy from you.
You don't sell at the seminar. You give the

attendees a reason to buy by appointment, in the following days after the seminar. A Gift Certificate is my favored method. A discount can be made, a Special package deal, a few free ads (if they commit to a longer contract) can be offered. But everyone must get the same offer. After the seminar, there is a form they fill out that asks: their name, contact information, what they learned, would they recommend the seminar to others, are they interested in more information. That way they can tell you in print (and in private) if they want to know more. And everyone is filling this out and handing it in. The other members of the audience will get the impression that most attendees are interested in advertising with you.

Immediately make the appointment.
If there are only a few at the seminar, just make the appointment right then and there. Certainly call the next day for the appointment, and try to get the appointment for the same day or next one. The longer you wait, the less effect the seminar has. If you call two weeks after the seminar... and they make the appointment two weeks after that... all the momentum of the seminar is gone.

Here's a tip; Call the attendees even if they didn't fill out an evaluation form, and hand it in. Call to thank them for attending ... or just stop by, and give them a Gift Certificate anyway. They will think it's just part of the program.

How often?
Even in the smallest market, you can do these seminars more than once a year. If you are serving a population of 100,000 or more I would recommend once a month until it gets hard to fill the room with twenty prospects. Then do it once a year.

Of course, the perfectly correct answer is "Repeat the seminar as often as it *produces a profit*, for as long as it is *still producing a profit*."

Should you do it yourself? Power of recognized third party.
Is your sales manager a good speaker? Some are. Then it's better to give the seminar yourself, because you can do it as often as you like. If you are a radio ad rep, and you have (or are) a celebrity radio personality... that's who should do the seminar. Prospects will come just to see and meet them. The two things you can sell are celebrity and authority. It amazes me how people regarded me differently after I wrote my first book on advertising. Having an author give your seminar will fill the room quicker and more easily. If you want someone who you can promote as an independent authority, I may be available. I will

customize the seminar to fit your media, and at the time of this writing, I don't even charge a speaking fee (under certain conditions).

Find out more about my speaking services, or doing it yourself at www.claudewhitacre.com

Recommended Reading;

Of course, you should have my book **The Unfair Advantage Small Business Advertising Manual**. Many of our ad rep clients give these as gifts to their prospects. The book effectively sells the client on the Return On Investment concept and Testing Their Ads, as well as how to make their advertising more profitable.

If you read it, you are getting a feel for what's in my 90 minute advertising seminar.

The Million Dollar Media Rep *by Michael Guld*
It's one of the only books on selling advertising that mentions how to create an ad that sells. There are some solid ideas there.

Successful Local Broadcast Sales *by Paul Weyland*
If you are selling radio or cable TV, this is the book to get. This guy knows his business, and you can transfer most of what he teaches to other media sales. And it's an absolute must to study. Both Weyland and Guld talk about studying advertising to put yourself ahead of the pack. See a pattern?

Marketing Your Retail Business *by Bob Negen*
A treasure trove of ideas to market at the retail level. Here's where you get ideas that you can share with your clients.

Influence *by Robert Cialdini*
The bible of how persuasion works.

Triggers *by Joe Sugarman*
The different appeals that he used in direct mail and print advertising. An absolute must.

High Probability Selling *by Jacques Werth and Nicholas Ruben*
If you want to cold call on the phone, and have a large market area, this book will show you how to do it without any fear of rejection. If you like the idea of only talking to people who are interested in talking to you, this book is for you.

Prospecting Your Way To Sales Success *by Bill Good*
Another excellent book on how to cold call on the phone. This book also teaches you how to handle objections on the phone. If you want to call to make appointments, this is the book to study.

Anything that John Caples writes
These are classics on writing ads that pay off. Get the first editions if possible. In later editions, all the comparable examples were taken out. These books were written in the 1930's to the 1950's. Don't let that turn you off. When these ads were written, the ad either sold, or the advertiser didn't eat. Devastatingly effective ad templates and examples.

Anything that Dan Kennedy writes
Kennedy knows more about marketing than anyone on the planet. He's prolific, brutally honest, and brilliant. This man makes me money every time I read his latest book. He doesn't write about selling advertising., but if you want to know how to motivate people to buy? He's the guy.

Additional Recommended Reading...

Media Selling: Television, Print, Internet, Radio
by Charles Warner

CA$HVERTISING: How to Use More than 100 Secrets of Ad-Agency Psychology to Make Big Money Selling Anything to Anyone
by Drew Eric Whitman

AdverSelling: How to Build Stronger Relationships and Close More Sales by Applying 26 Principles from Successful Advertising Campaigns
by James Hassett

Amazing Formulas Guarantee Advertising Sales
by Mark Charles Smalley

The Marketing and Sales Bible - (Selling is Human) – Advertising
by Lord N Highness W

The Guide to Selling Advertising Space, 2nd Edition
by Jack Bernstein

Selling Time: How to Sell small market radio advertising
by Dennis E. Brown

Selling Electronic Media
by Ed Shane

Ultimate Selling Power
by Donald J. Moine

Advertising and Promotion: An Integrated Marketing Communications Perspective
by George Belch and Michael Belch

Tested Advertising Methods (Prentice Hall Business Classics)
by John Caples and Fred E. Hahn

How to Make Your Advertising Make Money
by John Caples

Making Ads Pay: Timeless Tips for Successful Copywriting (Dover Books on History, Political and Social Science)
by John Caples

How To Write A Good Advertisement
by Victor O. Schwab and H. W. Hepner

My Life in Advertising and Scientific Advertising (Advertising Age Classics Library)
by Claude C. Hopkins

How I Raised Myself from Failure to Success in Selling
by Frank Bettger

Little Red Book of Selling: 12.5 Principles of Sales Greatness
by Jeffrey H. Gitomer

SPIN Selling
by Neil Rackham

How to Master the Art of Selling
by Tom Hopkins

The Psychology of Selling: Increase Your Sales Faster and Easier Than You Ever Thought Possible
by Brian Tracy

Services I provide;

I conduct the seminar **"How To Use Local Advertising To Survive And Thrive In Our Economy"** for business groups, trade organizations, and am available (schedule permitting) to conduct the seminar for your advertising clients. Go to www.claudewhitacre.com for more details. (If you are reading this after the recession is over, believe me, I've changed the seminar title)

One popular way to book me is for the entire day. I work with your reps, and give my **"Selling Local Advertising"** talk. This book acts as the text. Then in the evening, I conduct my seminar for your gathered group of clients and potential clients. If we follow a few simple guidelines, you will make an immediate profit... and also profit from the increased sales the seminar generates.

This book is available in quantity at attractive discounts. Advertising sales managers give a copy to every new hire. They tell us that the book shortens the learning curve, and makes their job of training easier. If fact, it was written with that in mind.

                                To Your Success,
                                      Claude

About The Author

Claude Whitacre is the author of the books **The Unfair Advantage Small Business Advertising Manual** and **Local Online Marketing**. Claude owns www.LocalProfitGeyser.com which offers a complete advertising service for local business owners to advertise properly. His methods drive ready buyers into their brick and mortar business or to the phone ready to buy.

Claude also owns a successful retail store, The Sweeper Store in Wooster, Ohio with his wife Cheryl. He uses the exact same marketing/advertising methods to promote his retail store as he teaches in this book. Claude's retail store has provided a lab to test marketing and advertising ideas for the past twelve years.

Claude divides his time between running his businesses, and speaking to groups of business owners about local online marketing and offline advertising strategies.

Claude and his wife Cheryl live quietly in the small college town of Wooster Ohio.

You can learn more about how Claude can help you at www.claudewhitacre.com

If you have enjoyed Selling Local Advertising, and want to take your sales to the next level, may I recommend my two latest books? One Call Closing gives you everything you need to know about how to get the sale today….not tomorrow. Stop wasting your time of endless callbacks, when you can have customers eager to buy from you today.

My book on sales prospecting, Sales Prospecting: The Ultimate Guide To Finding Highly Likely Prospects You Can Close In One Call, can show you all the most effective and painless ways I've found to see exactly the people you want to see…those who are highly likely to buy from you.

Did this book help you in your sales and marketing efforts? Through this book, you and I have shared an experience. I hope you enjoyed reading the book as much as I enjoyed writing it.

I'm going to ask you for a small favor.

If you would consider writing a review of this book on Amazon, I would very much appreciate it. The feedback I receive from readers will be helpful as I develop updates to this book and write other books for small business owners.

It will only take a minute, and your review will tell me and others what you got out of the book. Your review will help others decide if the book is for them.

To write a review of this book, just go to amazon.com and leave your review by clicking "Write a Customer Review" directly below the other reviews on my book page. You can also "Like" this book by visiting the detail page for the book and clicking the "Like" button under the title.

Review Questionnaire

If you're not sure how to write a review, other potential readers would probably appreciate your answers to these types of questions ...

- What have you learned from reading this book?
- Which section of the book did you find most useful?
- Would you recommend this book to a friend?
- A few lines, or a more in depth review...it's all up to you.

I really appreciate this.

Claude

Made in the USA
San Bernardino, CA
19 September 2017